EFFECTIVE DIGITAL LEARNING

TRANSFORMING TRADITIONAL LEARNING MODELS TO A VIRTUAL WORLD

Lisa Sims

Apress®

Effective Digital Learning: Transforming Traditional Learning Models to a Virtual World

Lisa Sims
Conyers, GA, USA

ISBN-13 (pbk): 978-1-4842-6863-6   ISBN-13 (electronic): 978-1-4842-6864-3
https://doi.org/10.1007/978-1-4842-6864-3

Copyright © 2021 by Lisa Sims

This work is subject to copyright. All rights are reserved by the Publisher, whether the whole or part of the material is concerned, specifically the rights of translation, reprinting, reuse of illustrations, recitation, broadcasting, reproduction on microfilms or in any other physical way, and transmission or information storage and retrieval, electronic adaptation, computer software, or by similar or dissimilar methodology now known or hereafter developed.

Trademarked names, logos, and images may appear in this book. Rather than use a trademark symbol with every occurrence of a trademarked name, logo, or image we use the names, logos, and images only in an editorial fashion and to the benefit of the trademark owner, with no intention of infringement of the trademark.

The use in this publication of trade names, trademarks, service marks, and similar terms, even if they are not identified as such, is not to be taken as an expression of opinion as to whether or not they are subject to proprietary rights.

While the advice and information in this book are believed to be true and accurate at the date of publication, neither the authors nor the editors nor the publisher can accept any legal responsibility for any errors or omissions that may be made. The publisher makes no warranty, express or implied, with respect to the material contained herein.

Managing Director, Apress Media LLC: Welmoed Spahr
Acquisitions Editor: Shiva Ramachandran
Development Editor: Matthew Moodie
Coordinating Editor: Nancy Chen

Cover designed by eStudioCalamar

Distributed to the book trade worldwide by Springer Science+Business Media New York, 1 New York Plaza, New York, NY 100043. Phone 1-800-SPRINGER, fax (201) 348-4505, e-mail orders-ny@springer-sbm.com, or visit www.springeronline.com. Apress Media, LLC is a California LLC and the sole member (owner) is Springer Science + Business Media Finance Inc (SSBM Finance Inc). SSBM Finance Inc is a **Delaware** corporation.

For information on translations, please e-mail booktranslations@springernature.com; for reprint, paperback, or audio rights, please e-mail bookpermissions@springernature.com.

Apress titles may be purchased in bulk for academic, corporate, or promotional use. eBook versions and licenses are also available for most titles. For more information, reference our Print and eBook Bulk Sales web page at http://www.apress.com/bulk-sales.

Any source code or other supplementary material referenced by the author in this book is available to readers on GitHub via the book's product page, located at www.apress.com/9781484268636. For more detailed information, please visit http://www.apress.com/source-code.

Printed on acid-free paper

This book is dedicated to all educators who work tirelessly especially during the Covid-19 pandemic to create a dynamic and creative digital learning environment and experience for all learners. Although it is not said or displayed nearly enough, you and your efforts are appreciated.

Contents

About the Author vii
Acknowledgments ix
Introduction xi

Chapter 1:   Emergence of Online Learning 1
Chapter 2:   Online Learning Equipment 9
Chapter 3:   Planning for Online Learning 19
Chapter 4:   Content Is King 27
Chapter 5:   Learning Management Systems 33
Chapter 6:   Presentation Tools 43
Chapter 7:   Webinars 55
Chapter 8:   Podcasts 67
Chapter 9:   Social Media Tools 79
Chapter 10: Blogs 87
Chapter 11: Free Online Resources 93
Chapter 12: Testing Online Learning 103
Chapter 13: Marketing Online Learning 109
Chapter 14: Before You Go 119

Index 123

About the Author

Lisa Sims is the Lead Faculty of Web and Mobile App Emphasis with Ashford University's Forbes School of Business and Technology. She has been teaching online in the area of Information Technology for over 20 years. Prior to joining Ashford University, Lisa worked as an adjunct faculty for the following online universities:

- University of Phoenix Online
- Southern New Hampshire
- Excelsior College

Lisa has worked in Information Technology in various roles such as programmer/analyst, web developer, and consultant.

When not teaching, she is an entrepreneur who loves to help other entrepreneurs start and grow their businesses via her blog, stretchingyourcash.com, and podcast, *Stretching a Dollar for Entrepreneurs*. She has a passion for using technology to work more efficiently and productively. Lisa is an Apress author and previously published the book *Building Your Online Store with WordPress and WooCommerce*. She is also the author of six other books which are available on Amazon.com and other online book retailers.

Lisa is active on social media and can be found on the following platforms:

- Facebook: www.facebook.com/stretchingadollar
- Twitter: www.twitter.com/bizmoneysaver
- Instagram: author_lisa_sims
- LinkedIn: www.linkedin.com/in/lisassims

Acknowledgments

I must first give God all the credit for giving me the idea to make this book possible. Writing a book during a pandemic is not an easy task, but God helped me to stay focused to meet my goal.

Special thanks and appreciation to Apress for giving me another opportunity to write another Apress book. I appreciate all the dedication and hard work of the Apress book team throughout the project. All the feedback was invaluable and contributed to bringing this book to fruition. Thank you, Matthew and Nancy, for making it a pleasant and memorable experience.

Most importantly, I want to thank my husband, Timothy Sr., and my two sons, Timothy Jr. and William, again for bearing with me as I worked on this project in the early morning hours during the Covid-19 pandemic. There is no perfect time to write a book, but if you put your mind to it, you can do it regardless of the situation.

Last but not least, thank you for making the investment in acquiring digital learning strategies to provide a positive and engaging learning experience for not only your learners but also yourself!

Introduction

Over the years, learning has remained the same. Although new methodologies have evolved, the general attitude toward learning has remained the same. If you ask most people what the best way is to learn, most people will probably say at a physical school. Over the last 10–20 years, more learning options emerged not only for learners but also educators. Learners and educators could choose between traditional in-person learning and online learning until March 2020.

During the middle of March 2020, a shift in learning occurred. As Covid-19 emerged and the number of cases started increasing, safety concerns arose. Since Covid-19 was a new virus, scientists and doctors had little to no information to refer to and did not know how to effectively prevent or treat it. To keep educators, learners, and school personnel safe, traditional, in-person learning transitioned online.

Since the decision to transition to digital or virtual learning happened so quickly and without adequate warning, many educators did not have enough time to properly prepare for it. Many educators only had experience teaching in traditional, in-person learning environments. Online learning was uncharted water. They utilized on-the-job training to figure out how to transform their traditional, in-person teaching skills to the digital or virtual environment. You might be in this group. Experienced online educators were looking to add new tools and strategies to their toolkits to engage learners. You might be in this group. Likewise, many learners did not have the necessities such as computers and Internet access to complete online learning. Needless to say, everyone became quickly frustrated.

Effective Digital Learning provides insights and resources to help both novice and experienced online educators thrive in the virtual learning environment. Each chapter offers practical information from an experienced online educator's perspective along with advice on how to apply it. Instead of searching the Web for this information, you have it in one place which helps save time. Some of the topics you will learn include:

- Emergence of online learning
- Online learning equipment
- Planning for online learning

Introduction

- Planning content
- Learning management systems
- Presentation tools
- Webinars
- Free learning resources

After the pandemic is over, digital learning will still remain. The information in this book will be applicable and promote effective digital learning. As we all know, learners are the most important component in the learning process. They deserve your best. This book will allow you not only to provide the best to them but also to yourself. You and your learners will benefit greatly from this book. I would love to hear from you. Please feel free to follow me on social media and let me know how you enjoyed the book.

Let's get started!

CHAPTER 1

Emergence of Online Learning

When most people hear the word "learning" or "education," their minds immediately imagine a school where students are sitting at desks listening intently to a teacher. Most people experienced this model throughout their lifetime. Public education in the United States, Canada, and Australia has been defined as "federally funded school, administered to some extent by the government, and charged with educating all citizens."[1] The public education definition included the following schools:

- Primary and secondary schools
- Public universities

Public education is free. To appreciate how far public education has progressed, it is always good to review its history.

History of Public Education

National Geographic reports that on April 23, 1635, the Boston Latin School became the first public school formed in Boston, Massachusetts.[2] It still exists today. According to EducationBug.org, in 1647, the General Court of

---

[1] www.educationbug.org/a/history-of-public-schools.html
[2] www.nationalgeographic.org/thisday/apr23/first-public-school-america/

© Lisa Sims 2021
L. Sims, *Effective Digital Learning*, https://doi.org/10.1007/978-1-4842-6864-3_1

Massachusetts Bay Colony responded to a decree for the need for elementary and Latin schools and created schools that were a mixture of public and private schools that were available to everyone but taught Puritan values and Bible reading.[3] Although most learning took place at home, only the privileged social economic class sent their sons to physical in-person Latin schools. Fast forward almost a decade later, Massachusetts created a law requiring townships with 50 or more people to hire a teacher to teach the town's children basic academics. Towns with 100 or more people were required to have an elementary school to teach reading, writing, and religion. For many years, it was the primary way to learn and acquire new knowledge, while others learned skills through apprenticeships. In the mid-1800s, people in Massachusetts demanded free, compulsory education for all children. It took until 1851 for this to happen.

Although compulsory education was available in Massachusetts, other educational battles were being fought in the South. During the Reconstruction Era, African Americans fought for public education. Other states also fought their battles. As a result of the US Supreme Court Case *Plessy v. Ferguson* decision, public education was required to be legally segregated. According to EducationBug.org, the US Supreme Court decision in *Brown v. Board of Education of Topeka* in 1954 ruled that segregated schools were unequal and must be abolished. It took a Federal court ruling in 1957 requiring public schools in Little Rock, Arkansas, to be integrated.

Evolution of Education

Distance learning first occurred in the 1800s. Initially, distance learning resembled correspondence courses where students worked on preassigned lessons that were received and returned to professors via US Postal Service mail. With correspondence courses, the interaction between students and teachers was limited and feedback was delayed. With materials being sent via US Postal Service mail, they could have easily been incomplete or lost. Over the years, distance learning has transformed into these forms:

- Telecourses
- CD-ROM courses
- Online learning
- Mobile learning

As time progressed and technological advances such as computers and the Internet became available, another learning option emerged: online learning. Online learning, also called eLearning or virtual learning, uses the Internet to

---

[3]www.educationbug.org/a/history-of-public-schools.html

create an online classroom. The classroom is typically through a cloud-based learning management system (LMS), where teachers and students engage with the class materials. It transitioned the traditional physical classroom to an online environment using technology to simulate in-person interaction. Online learning is a type of distance learning.

Today, online learning via computer or mobile device is the most popular form of distance learning. Compared to traditional distance learning, online learning significantly increased student and teacher interaction. In addition, course materials are immediately available to students rather than waiting to receive them via US Postal Service mail. Students also receive feedback quicker and in various forms such as email, video, audio, or text.

The first online learning occurred in 1989, when the University of Phoenix used CompuServe, one of the first consumer online services, to offer its educational programs. In 1990, Tim Berners-Lee created the first web browser called WorldWideWeb. Three years later, the web browser Mosaic was created. Until this point, most web browsers were text-based. Mosaic was the first web browser that allowed images to be embedded in HTML pages and displayed to users. As the capabilities of web browsers advanced, online learning began to grow. According to EducationData.org, in 2017, a total of 19.7 million students enrolled in courses at degree-granting postsecondary institutions, of which 6.6 million enrolled in some form of distance education/online learning courses.[4] As these numbers indicate, online learning is not a new trend. It continues to increase as technology advances.

Why Should You Care?

Today, almost any corporation that sells a product or service offers some type of online learning training to its employees, customers, or potential customers as opposed to only primary, secondary, postsecondary, and training institutions. If you conduct a Google search on the term "online learning," as in Figure 1-1, you will receive over 2 billion results for all types of online learning organizations.

---

[4] https://educationdata.org/online-education-statistics/

Chapter 1 | Emergence of Online Learning

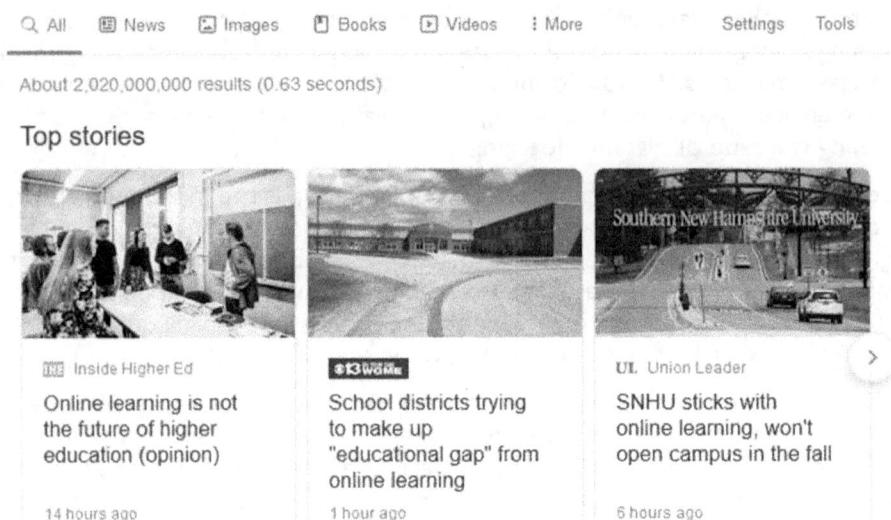

Figure 1-1. Google search results for the term "online learning"

Regardless of your age, ability, or skill set, online learning provides many benefits to today's learners and instructors.

Online Learning Benefits

For those who are new to online learning, the adjustment can be difficult. It is a different way of learning compared to what many have experienced. Change is never easy but sometimes necessary. Let us look at some of the benefits of online learning.

Flexibility

Unlike traditional learning that occurs on designated days and times, most online learning is asynchronous. Asynchronous means there is not a dedicated time that teachers and learners must attend classes. However, there might be a certain number of required days to meet attendance and participation requirements. Most people are looking for ways to find work/life balance in their lives, and with online learning's flexibility, learners and teachers can set their schedules.

Time-Saver

Time is one of the most valuable assets that we have. Everyone has 24 hours in a day and makes the most of them. Once they are gone, they are gone forever. With busy schedules, everyone is looking for ways to save more time to do more things. Online learning allows learners and teachers to save by using the Internet rather than sitting in traffic.

Money Saver

In addition to being a time-saver, online learning can also be a money saver for online learners and teachers. For online learners, some online learning and course costs can be less expensive than traditional in-person courses. Other than public primary and secondary education, which have their inherent fees, many postsecondary institutions and other on-site training can be expensive. Eliminating travel to a brick-and-mortar building can help learners and teachers save money on gas, parking, lodging, food, and other costs.

Classroom Anywhere

Online learning allows learners and teachers to create a virtual classroom anytime and anywhere an Internet connection and a computer or mobile device are available. Traditional education required learners to rearrange their lives around attending a physical school. Online learning requires and creates a paradigm shifting in thinking and allows learners to arrange their education in conjunction with their lives. An excellent example of this is the Covid-19 pandemic. When schools and other learning institutions were forced to close their doors due to the pandemic, learning shifted online. By moving learning online, learners, teachers, and other school administrators were still able to learn while being protected from the potential coronavirus spread.

Another example is the active duty military. Military personnel are often deployed all over the world. Still, they continue to use online learning to complete their educational goals. Otherwise, they could not resume their education until their deployments are completed.

Mobile Learning

Advances in mobile device technology and their increasing screen sizes along with less expensive options such as Chromebooks and Android tablets have made it easier for online learners to connect than in previous years. According to Pew Internet Research, the percentage of people who owned smartphones increased from 35% in 2011 to 81% in 2019.[5] It went on to state that in 2019, 96% of people owned smartphones.

Online Learning Considerations

With all of its benefits, online learning might appear to be the solution for all situations. However, that is not always the case. There are some online learning considerations that must be considered.

Digital Divide

Although we are living in the 21st century, not all people have access to high-speed Internet access. For example, some rural areas still struggle to obtain reliable, high-speed Internet access. Their current Internet service is either too slow or nonexistent. As a result, it is difficult for them to further their learning.

Quality

Is online learning comparable to in-person learning? Are learners learning? Can technology be used as an effective medium to replicate pedagogy in the education model? These questions and others will be asked as more and more primary, secondary, and postsecondary schools and learning organizations implement online learning. Online learning might never completely replace the traditional learning model. As technology advances, tools such as web conferencing and virtual reality provide a viable alternative.

---

[5]www.pewresearch.org/internet/fact-sheet/mobile/

Special Needs Learners

Some special needs learners are not able to do online learning. Based on their disability and its severity, it might not be as beneficial as in-person learning. For example, teletherapy services such as occupational and speech therapy are conducted online. For learners that require more hands-on instruction, online learning might not be the right fit, but it is still accessible to those who can use it.

Summary

Online learning will continue to evolve along with technology. As the workforce continues to need more knowledge workers, it will become easier for learners to gain the skills they need at their convenience. It will also be affordable. For educators, the opportunities to share and present their expertise will be limitless.

CHAPTER 2

Online Learning Equipment

As you learned in the previous chapter, the traditional brick-and-mortar learning environment has been transformed by online learning. Traditional learning is no longer the only option available to learners and educators. Over the years, online learning has given learners the flexibility to learn new skills at their convenience using whatever medium was available at the time. It also allowed educators to teach on their schedules. Today, the Internet is the primary online learning medium. A physical classroom environment is no longer the only option which helps remove some educational barriers. You might be eager to become an online learner or online educator but are unsure of the necessary equipment needs. What do you need to get started?

Technology Needs

Whether you want to be an online learner or an online educator, your success depends on one critical component: technology. Technology is at the heart of online learning. It is the conduit through which learning happens. Without the right technology, you will not be as productive or efficient. Likewise, you will also waste valuable time and money. As a result, you will not receive the benefits that online learning offers. The good news is that the technology that is needed for online learning is minimal.

Chapter 2 | Online Learning Equipment

Hardware

Although you do not need to have the newest computer, it still needs to be no more than 2–4 years old. Computer technology changes rapidly, so what is current today will be obsolete in about 2–5 years. Most learning institutions provide learners and educators with hardware requirements to work with their technology infrastructure. A good rule to follow is to have an operational desktop or laptop computer that is 2–3 years old with the following minimum specifications:

- Windows 7 operating system or Mac 10.2 Sierra operating system or higher
- Intel i3 dual-core processor or AMD equivalent or higher
- 2 GHZ processor or higher
- 1 GB of free disk space
- 4GB of memory or higher
- Webcam

You can use an older computer. However, it will affect the performance of your online learning experience. The higher your processor speed and memory are, the more applications can be opened simultaneously. Your computer will also operate faster.

Chromebooks are smaller laptops with smaller screens that operate Google's operating system, Chrome OS. Typically, they are less expensive than desktops and laptops and utilize Google's cloud-based applications such as Gmail and Google Drive. Due to their slow processor speed and a small amount of memory, they should not be the primary choice for postsecondary online learning involving programming or other processor-intensive courses. However, they are a good choice for primary and secondary learners. Another Chromebook limitation is that they cannot operate without Internet access.

As the size of mobile devices continues to increase, they will continue to add to the flexibility of traditional and online learning. Many learning resources are available as apps via these devices. Notification apps such as Remind and Show My Homework can help educators communicate not only with students but also parents. Some mobile devices can be more expensive than desktops or laptops. They also lack a physical keyboard. It must be purchased separately. Lastly, they are limited in their processing speed and memory. Due to their portability, they can be great to use to supplement learning on the go.

Printer

Although most of your online learning occurs online, you will have times where you will want to print documents. Having an inkjet or laser printer allows you to print when needed. The initial cost of an inkjet printer can be less than a laser printer. However, laser printers can print more pages with their toner compared to inkjets. Today, many all-in-one printers are available that include a scanner, which can save you money and space.

Scanner

Having a scanner is good to have but not a necessity. If you do not have a scanner, do not fret. Many scanning apps are available for free and a fee on mobile devices. For instance, the Notes app is freely available on iOS devices and allows you to scan documents.

Software

The main software that you will need is a web browser such as Firefox, Safari, Edge, or Google Chrome. A web browser is typically how learning materials are accessed. In addition to a web browser, you will need some additional software.

Microsoft 365

Microsoft Office is the industry standard application for schools and organizations. It allows you to create documents, presentations, spreadsheets, and more using its popular programs such as Word, PowerPoint, and Excel. It also contains Microsoft Outlook for email and OneNote for cloud-based storage needs. For primary, secondary, and postsecondary students and educators with an email address ending in .edu, Microsoft 365 can be downloaded for free from the Microsoft website (Figure 2-1). Subscription information is available on the Microsoft website.

Chapter 2 | Online Learning Equipment

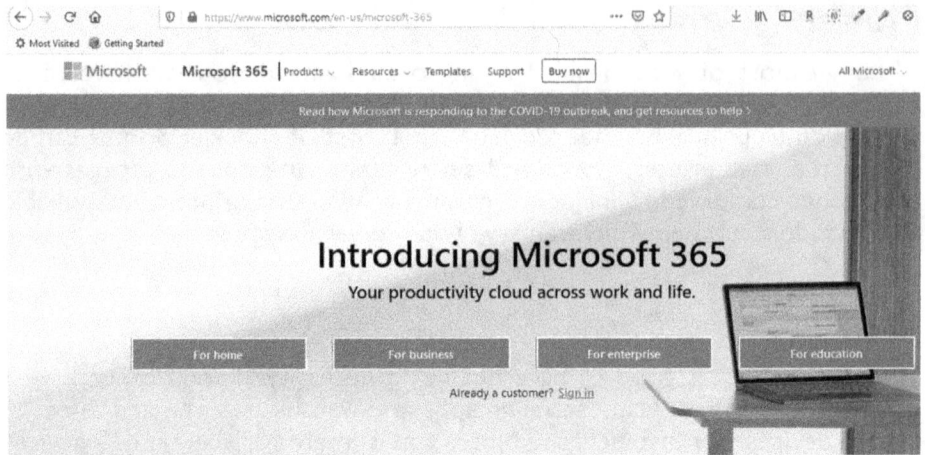

Figure 2-1. Microsoft website for Microsoft 365

Also, Microsoft 365 and Google Docs apps are freely available to use in the Apple App Store and Google Play Store. Many cloud-based applications make it easier to use these applications on computers and mobile devices. However, without a paid Microsoft 365 subscription, the functionality is limited.

Antivirus Software

Since you will be working on the Web and uploading and downloading files, it is a good idea to have antivirus software installed on your computer or mobile device. Antivirus software protects your computer from viruses and other threats that can infect your computer or mobile device and cause harm. Once antivirus software is installed, it should be programmed to automatically update itself to protect your computer or device from new threats that arise daily. A few popular free antivirus software options that also include paid options include

- Avast – www.avast.com
- AVG – www.avg.com

Other popular paid antivirus options include

- McAfee – www.mcafee.com
- Norton – www.norton.com

PDF Reader

PDFs are the standard document type used on the Web. They can be viewed on all devices as long as a program such as Adobe Acrobat Reader is installed. Adobe Acrobat Reader is the industry standard for viewing PDFs and is free for download from the Adobe website (Figure 2-2).

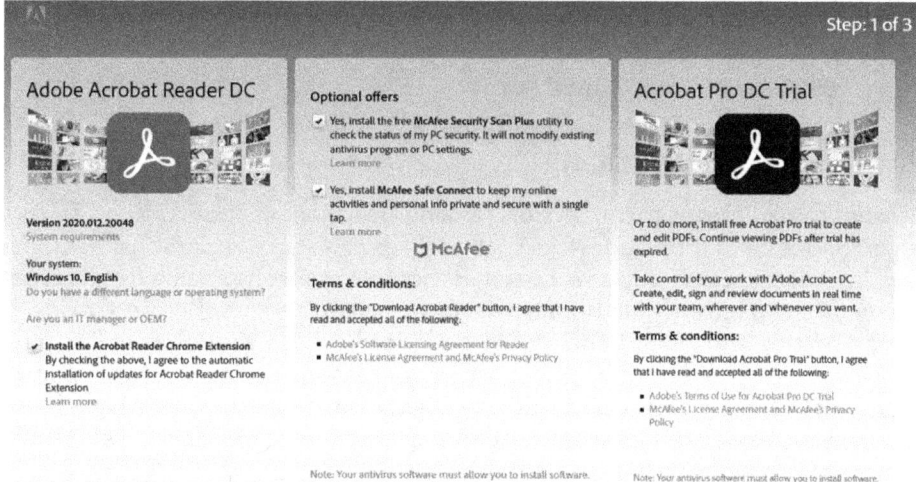

Figure 2-2. Adobe Acrobat Reader available for free download from Adobe website: https://get.adobe.com/reader/

Cloud-Based Storage

Since online learning provides the flexibility to work from anywhere, you need access to your files from anywhere and from any device. Cloud-based storage can also be used to back up important files. Some popular cloud-based storage options include

- Microsoft OneDrive (comes with Microsoft Office 365)
- Dropbox – www.dropbox.com
- Google Drive – www.google.com/drive/

Graphic Design Software

In addition to your typical software needs, you might require graphic design software to create graphics for videos, websites, photography, and more. For your graphic design needs, the Adobe Creative Cloud consists of industry standard apps such as Photoshop and InDesign and is available at www.adobe.com. It contains desktop and mobile apps for your creative needs. You can purchase either individual apps or all Adobe apps for a monthly or yearly subscription fee. Teachers and students with valid proof of eligibility (i.e., school ID or school email address) receive discounts on the purchase price.

Although Adobe Creative Suite is great for graphic design, it can be expensive. Some free and open source graphic design software include the following:

- Gimp – www.gimp.org
- Canva – www.canva.com

Internet Connection

Without an Internet connection, online learning cannot occur. Today's smartphones and mobile devices such as iPads can serve as personal hotspots for Internet access, but the speed is not always comparable to Internet connection speeds in our homes, libraries, or restaurants. Before Covid-19, local libraries and restaurants could be visited to use the Internet for free. However, many closed their doors for safety reasons during the pandemic. In many communities and rural areas, the Digital Divide exists where high-speed Internet or broadband Internet is neither available nor affordable. As a result, many are left without Internet access.

Since today's online learning consists of multimedia and other resources, a high-speed Internet connection is required. According to www.reviews.org, a high-speed Internet connection is one in which the download speed is of a minimum of 25 Mbps.[1] The number of US households with high-speed Internet has increased from 65% in 2018 to 73% in 2019.[2]

Accessories

Now that you know your core hardware and software requirements needs, there are some necessary accessories you will want to purchase. These accessories will allow for a better online learning experience.

Headset with Microphone

Depending on your environment, it is always a good idea to have a headset with a microphone. A headset allows you to review multimedia content privately without relying on your device's speakers. You also will not disturb

---

[1] www.reviews.org/internet-service/what-is-high-speed-internet/
[2] www.pewresearch.org/internet/2019/06/13/mobile-technology-and-home-broadband-2019/

others around you. For learning activities that require you to use your voice, a headset with noise cancelling microphone is a good investment. It can filter out background noise and allow your audience to hear you loudly and clearly. Most computers and mobile devices are equipped with internal microphones. However, they are directional and pick up all background noise in a room rather than filtering or reducing it. They also do not provide good voice quality compared to external microphones.

An external headset with noise cancelling microphone is not expensive. It averages around $40 but increases in price based on the noise cancelling level. Whatever headset you select, pay attention to whether it uses a USB, lightning port, or 3.5mm plug for your device (Figure 2-3).

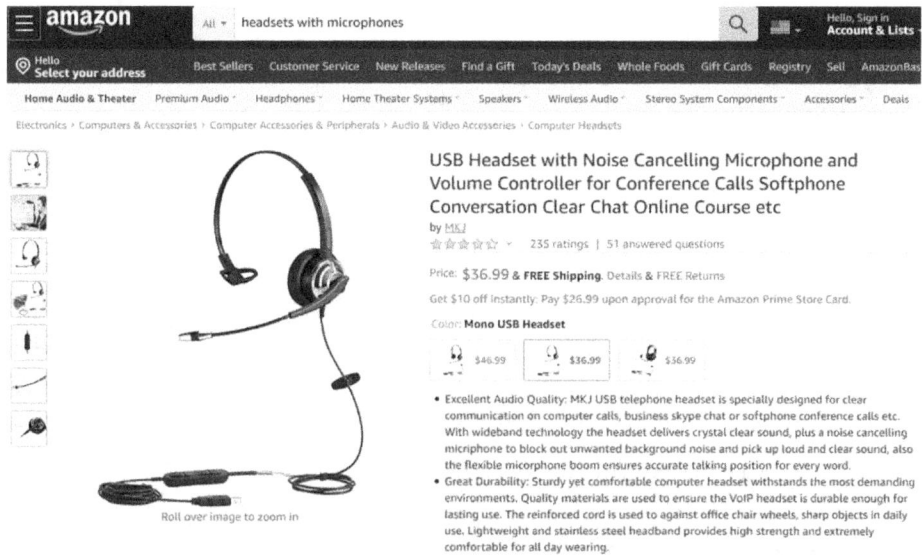

Figure 2-3. USB headset for computers for online learning available from Amazon.com

For iPhone users, Apple's EarPods with lightning connector is also another option (Figure 2-4). It also has a 3.5mm adapter option which can also be used on computers, and on later model iPhones and iPads as well as other mobile devices. Most smartphones come with headphones with a microphone that can be used until you find a replacement. Although the Apple EarPods have a microphone, they do not provide noise cancelling.

Chapter 2 | Online Learning Equipment

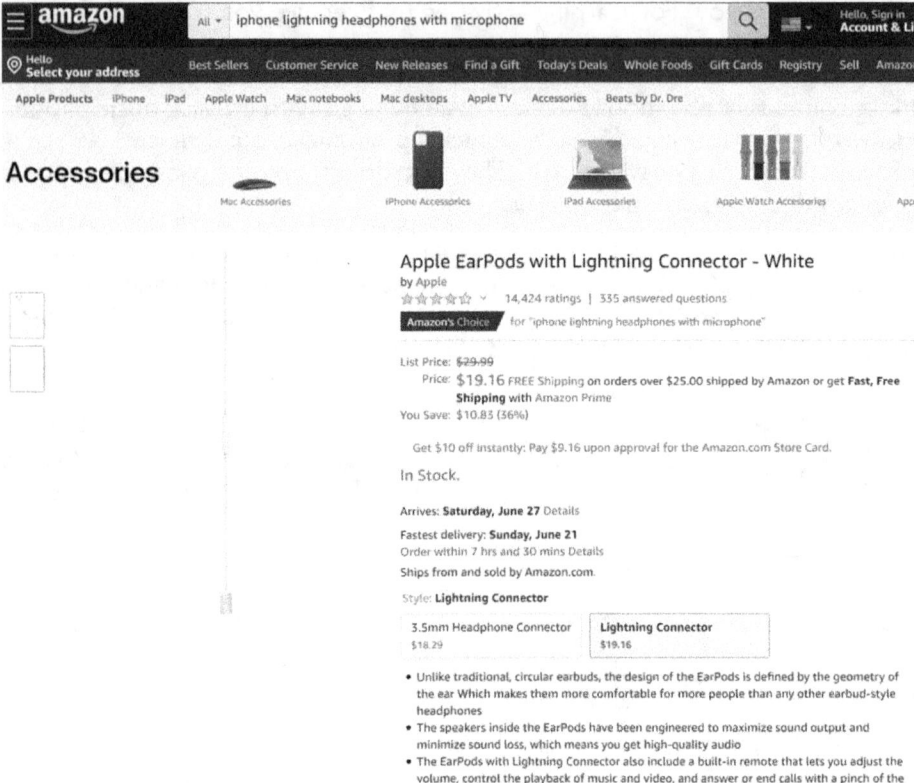

Figure 2-4. Apple's EarPod headset option for online learning

Webcam

Although a webcam is optional for some online learning, it is a nice complement. Most computers and mobile devices come equipped with a webcam. For learners, it brings a face-to-face component of traditional learning to the online classroom. For educators, a webcam provides many benefits. First, it allows educators to record their course content and share it within the virtual classroom. The content can also be repurposed and shared on various social media platforms. A webcam lets educators make a personal connection with their learners. When learners can put a face with a name, it can relieve some of the isolation and anxiety of online learning.

If you do not have a webcam, your mobile device's camera will work. Most mobile device cameras have a high resolution that can not only take great pictures but also record videos. For example, the newer iPhones after iPhone 7 have superior cameras that can be used to not only take pictures but also create videos. The same goes for the new model iPads. If you use either of these, you will need to purchase a tripod to hold the device steady.

Summary

As we have seen, the technology equipment needs for online learning are minimal. Many of these items you probably already have, which saves you time and money. It also helps to resolve some of the myths you might had heard about getting started with online learning. Trying anything for the first time can seem like a daunting task, but you can do it. With the right equipment, your journey can begin with a positive start. In the next chapter, you will explore how to successfully plan for your online learning journey. As the old adage goes, "If you fail to plan, you plan to fail." You will have a plan.

CHAPTER 3

Planning for Online Learning

In the previous chapter, we explored the online learning technology needs for students and educators. Without the proper technology, educators and students can experience unnecessary frustrations that could have been prevented. Although technology is at the heart of the online learning experience, other critical components are involved. Planning helps educators utilize the various online learning technology components to create the optimal learning experience for learners.

Planning involves looking at the bigger picture and determining what individual pieces of the online learning environment will work together to benefit learners. Without a well-thought-out plan of how all the pieces work together, online learning can be difficult and not produce the desired outcomes for educators and students. As the old adage goes, *"If you fail to plan, you plan to fail."* A detailed plan can be the difference between success and failure. Before you can devise a plan, you must determine your purpose.

Purpose

Having a clear purpose keeps you focused on your goal. In traditional learning, many educators utilize a lesson plan to structure their days and keep them focused. Although the learning environment is different due to Covid-19, the method is still the same. You must have a plan and a purpose. Purpose fuels your drive and drives your day. Throughout a typical learning day, you will be pulled in different directions, so having a clearly defined purpose reduces your chances of becoming distracted. Online learning is not easy for educators or students particularly during a pandemic. It is unchartered territory that everyone is learning to navigate daily. Having a clear purpose provides a road map that you can follow to keep you on track or adjust as needed. Some possible questions to ask yourself to determine your purpose include:

- What outcomes do you want to accomplish?
- Why are you teaching online?
- Why is online teaching important to you?
- What do you hope to accomplish through online learning?

Once you answer these questions, you should jot them down either in a journal or on your favorite note-taking mobile app such as Evernote or Microsoft OneNote to periodically review. They will serve as your daily motivation. Now that you are clear on your purpose, there are some other factors you should consider.

Online Learning Organization

Organizing your learning materials is an important step that is often overlooked in online learning. Without an intuitive organization system, you can waste valuable time trying to locate learning resources. As you are creating your learning resources, you want to make sure that you give them descriptive names and save them in descriptive folders on your computer. It is also a good practice to back up your learning resources to a cloud-based system such as Microsoft OneDrive or Google Drive.

Although your learning management system will already have an organization structure in place, you want to make sure that the learning resources you add are intuitive for your learners to find the necessary materials. Nothing frustrates learners more than not being able to easily locate something in the online learning environment. Always think about your audience first before creating any learning resources to guarantee the best possible outcomes.

Mindset

One of the hardest things to change is our mindset on certain things. No one likes to change but it is inevitable. Benjamin Franklin's quote sums up how most people feel about life's certainties: *In this world, nothing is certain except death and taxes.* When we encounter something new or a change from the norm, it can scare us. As we have seen with Covid-19, the things once considered normal in all areas of our lives no longer exist. Everything has changed and we must adapt. Oftentimes, it is the fear of the unknown more than the change itself that scares us.

Online learning might be out of your comfort zone. When you compare a new concept to a familiar concept, apprehension can easily set in. Many educators have been thrust into the online learning paradigm without any training and are figuring it out as they go along. For many, the traditional learning paradigm has been embedded in their minds and lives for years. It is the only learning model most know and have taught. Other educators were already familiar with online learning and looking for ways to improve their skills.

When online learning originated as another alternative to traditional learning, many in the education space were skeptical because it was a change from the norm. It was not familiar to them. They could not understand how learning could occur outside a physical classroom. For some, it can be difficult to overcome these feelings which can cause them to miss out on the opportunities for online learning. Regardless of the medium used, learning still can occur. Some resources to help influence your mindset while increasing your online teaching skills and knowledge include:

- Corwin – https://us.corwin.com/en-us/nam/online-teaching-toolkit
- Future Learn – www.futurelearn.com/info/blog/resources-for-online-teaching-during-coronavirus
- eLearning Industry – https://elearningindustry.com/
- Edutopia – www.edutopia.org/
- Faculty Focus – www.facultyfocus.com

Being able to overcome these feelings as an educator is crucial. These feelings can indirectly and directly influence your attitude toward online learning and appear within your online learning delivery silently sabotaging your efforts. Online learning should not be viewed as a replacement for traditional learning. Instead, it should be viewed as an addition. Everyone learns differently and excels in a delivery method that caters to their learning style. Keeping an open and positive mindset motivates you to put forth your best teaching efforts to help students effectively learn.

Time Management

Everyone has 24 hours in a day. Within those 24 hours, we juggle daily responsibilities that might or might not get accomplished. Once those hours are gone, we cannot reclaim them. We must start again the next day. Compared to traditional learning, online learning does not have standard school hours which requires better time management skills. Contrary to what many believe, online learning requires a lot of preparation and effort. Oftentimes, it can seem as if your workday never ends while trying to balance your learners' needs along with your professional and personal needs. At times, it can seem overwhelming. Without the preplanned daily schedule offered by traditional learning, it can become easy to forget things while organizing your teaching schedule.

Online learning offers flexibility that can complement work/life balance. However, many educators are still overwhelmed with life's tasks. During Covid-19, many educators have children they must assist with online learning in conjunction with teaching online. Some also might be caregivers or dealing with personal health issues. Attendance and participation requirements exist for educators in both traditional and online learning modalities that they must adhere to while learning how to stay safe and teach in this new normal. It is not easy to juggle. Although you might already have a scheduling tool, it never hurts to have options.

Google Calendar is a free online calendaring system used for scheduling appointments and other important events. You can think of it as an online planner with time management capabilities. Not only can these events be seen online, but they can also be saved to your mobile device's calendar (Figure 3-1). By utilizing a calendaring system such as Google Calendar, you can schedule lesson prep time, assignment due dates, office hours, and more without missing something. Since it is cloud-based and available with a Gmail account, it can be viewed on any device. Likewise, the Google Calendar app can be downloaded to iOS and Android mobile devices.

Effective Digital Learning | 23

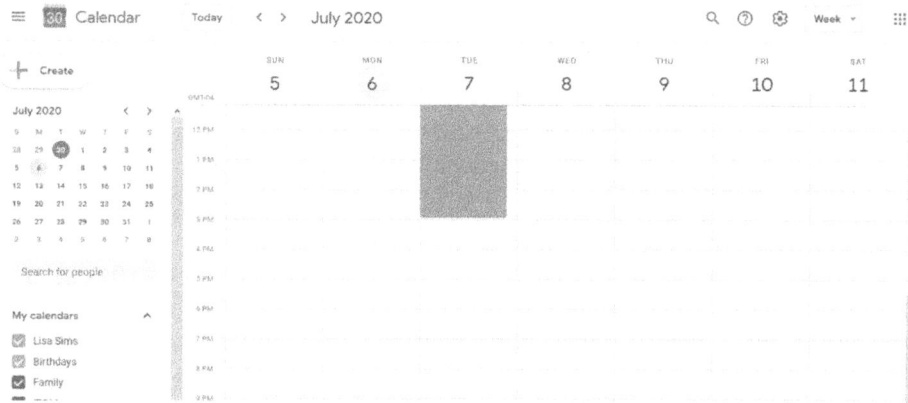

Figure 3-1. Google Calendar that can be used for appointments and reminders

Another alternative is to use your mobile device's calendar. Since many of us always have our mobile devices with us all the time, we can easily schedule events and receive notifications. You can even set a reminder several days in advance to notify you of meetings, office hours, and grading deadlines.

Microsoft To Do is another tool to add to your teaching toolbox. It can be used as a personal planner to create to-do lists and reminders to help you stay focused and organized throughout your day. It is free and available to use via the Web and as an app on Windows, Android, and iOS platforms (Figure 3-2).

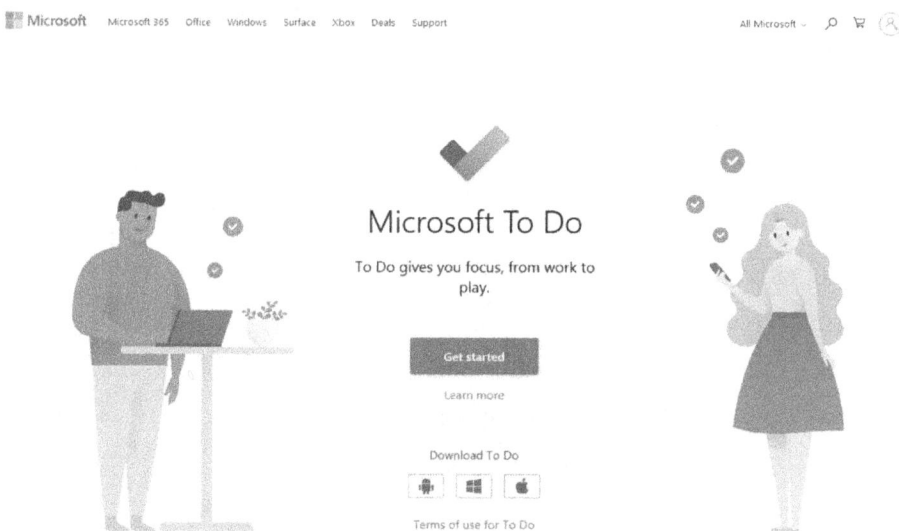

Figure 3-2. Microsoft To Do allows you to create to-do lists to stay organized and focused

Work Area

Although online learning allows you to work or teach from anywhere, a designated teaching area can increase your productivity. Once you enter into this space, your mind and body know that teaching will occur similar to entering a physical classroom. A teaching area also reduces distractions and keeps you focused.

Everyone has heard the saying that a cluttered workspace represents a cluttered mind. In some ways, it is true. Clutter can affect us not only consciously but also subconsciously. According to Psychology Today, clutter can cause our thinking to not be as sharp as it should.[1] Clutter can also heighten our stress and anxiety levels. Having a clutter-free teaching work area prepares and motivates you for success. A clutter-free area projects a professional image during web conferencing sessions. Although these might seem like small items, they can add up to make a big impact on your teaching success.

Social Media Support

Sometimes, online learning can feel isolating. However, it does not have to be. There are numerous online groups that you can join for assistance with teaching in an online learning environment. For instance, Facebook has numerous groups and pages that you can join or follow to gain new insights and resources about online learning. Likewise, you can also network with other online educators. Some Facebook Pages you might want to follow include:

- Global Online Academy
- TED-Ed
- Global Educator Collective
- edX
- Khan Academy

Facebook groups that you might want to join include:

- Digital Resources for Distance Learning
- Distance Learning Educators
- Online Teaching Strategies for Educators

---

[1] www.psychologytoday.com/us/blog/fulfillment-any-age/201705/5-reasons-clear-the-clutter-out-your-life

LinkedIn is another good social media resource that offers groups that you can join to not only network but also learn new online learning strategies.

Self-Care

Educators tend to put the needs of their students before their own. With online learning, you can easily put in more hours on a computer or mobile device than in-person traditional learning. Sometimes, you must be a little selfish. You must always remember the saying "*You cannot pour from an empty cup.*" Take care of yourself and schedule some time for some self-care to recharge and regroup. Otherwise, you will quickly suffer from burnout. Some simple self-care tips include:

- Schedule some daily exercise such as a walk or yoga
- Establish consistent work hours
- Eat healthy
- Drink plenty of water
- Get enough rest
- Take breaks throughout the day

Summary

Online learning involves more than technology. You must have a well-thought-out plan to serve as your road map. However, you will need to adjust your plan as needed. A quote from Robert Burns' "To A Mouse" sums up how you should view plans: *The best-laid plans of mice and men often go awry.*

No matter how carefully a project is planned, something may still go wrong with it. Be flexible.

CHAPTER 4

Content Is King

In Chapter 3, you learned about the importance of planning and its role in the online learning experience. Planning prepares the foundation for a good outcome for both educators and learners. However, it does not always guarantee a positive teaching and learning outcome. Unexpected circumstances will occur such as Covid-19, and contingencies will have to be made. However, planning does help begin the online learning journey on a positive note. With a good understanding of the planning process, you can start brainstorming and planning your online learning content.

We have all heard the expression "content is king," and in no place is this truer than in online learning. Since there is not a physical teacher and classroom in online learning as in traditional learning, content must be planned and designed carefully. Depending on the quality and delivery, content can make or break an online learning experience. It also must be composed of many different learning components. Otherwise, it might not provide the intended benefits which can result in failure.

Content Basics

Content is at the core of any online learning experience. It consists of learning objectives and outcomes that learners complete along a designated path. While studying the subject matter, learners interact with the content. In academia, traditional and online learning typically follows some form of pedagogy. Merriam-Webster defines pedagogy as "the art, science, or

© Lisa Sims 2021
L. Sims, *Effective Digital Learning*, https://doi.org/10.1007/978-1-4842-6864-3_4

profession of teaching."[1] Pedagogy works together with the content to achieve learning objectives and goals.

Many different content elements are used to fulfill online learning pedagogy. Previously, written lectures inserted into learning management systems or posted on a designated website paired with ebooks were the primary methods of delivering online course content. Besides quizzes and tests, there was not a way to analyze whether the learning materials were effective. With technology innovations and creative thinking, content creation has greatly evolved. Written lectures have now been paired with the following:

- Videos
- Podcasts
- Internet articles
- Blog posts
- PowerPoints
- Prezis

Today, content is organized to promote not only critical and analytical thinking but also learner engagement. In the upcoming chapters, you will explore specific applications and apps to help you create various types of content.

Although content can have various formats, its focus must keep learners and their needs as the top priority. Learners are the most important stakeholders of the online learning equation. Before creating any content, learners and their learning styles should always be considered (Figure 4-1).

---

[1] www.merriam-webster.com/dictionary/pedagogy

Effective Digital Learning

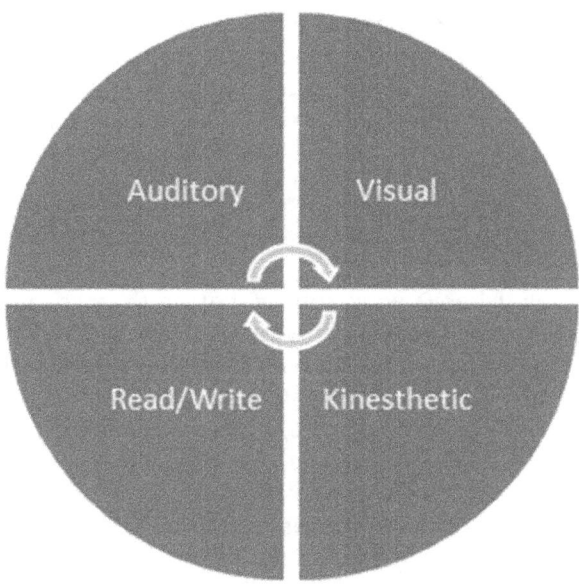

Figure 4-1. The four learning types of learners

Unfortunately, there is not a one-size-fits-all content for all learners. All learners do not learn the same. For instance, some learners have disabilities such as hearing or vision impairments and require accessibility accommodations (Figure 4-2). An accessibility accommodation example is including captions and transcripts within videos for learners with visual impairments that utilize screen readers. Failing to consider these learners when creating your content could potentially exclude them from your online learning experience.

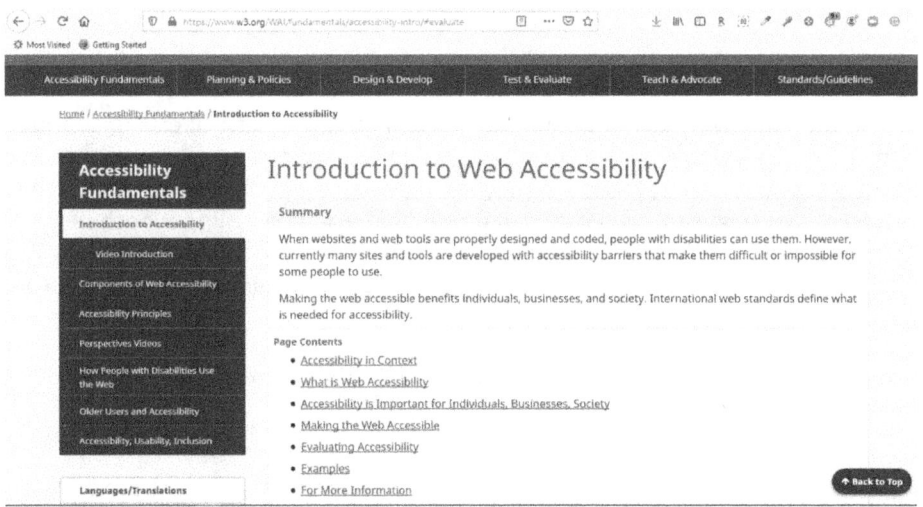

Figure 4-2. The W3C provides information about making website content accessible

Content should also be scannable. Most people do not like to read long paragraphs of text along with long sentences on any sized screen. It can be intimidating. Using bullets is a good technique to make content scannable. Utilizing white space between paragraphs is another way to make scannable content.

Content Purpose

As an educator, you know your subject better than anyone. You are the primary content creator and subject matter expert and know which learning materials will work or not. New learning resources are released all the time. Depending on your budget and available resources, you might be tempted to purchase some of these. Although they might supplement your content, you have some important decisions to make. For instance, many of these materials can range in price from free to expensive. Regardless of their price, learning materials must serve a primary purpose: facilitate student learning. Content and materials that provide the latest bells and whistles might look great, but you must be willing to ask yourself the following questions:

- Will it help students understand the material better?
- Will it encourage students to use their critical thinking skills?
- Will it add value to the content as well as students?

Considering content without considering learners would be like painting in the dark. You will get the paint on the walls, but it will not look good when you turn on the lights. Never lose sight of the primary purpose of your content.

Content Goals

It is important to determine your content's goals. Thinking like your learners is one way to establish content goals. Asking questions of your content is a good technique to evaluate whether it will meet learner's needs and expectations (Figure 4-3). Likewise, it will help you determine whether it will help you reach your course outcomes. The order of these questions is not important. What is important is that they help you brainstorm your content goals.

Effective Digital Learning

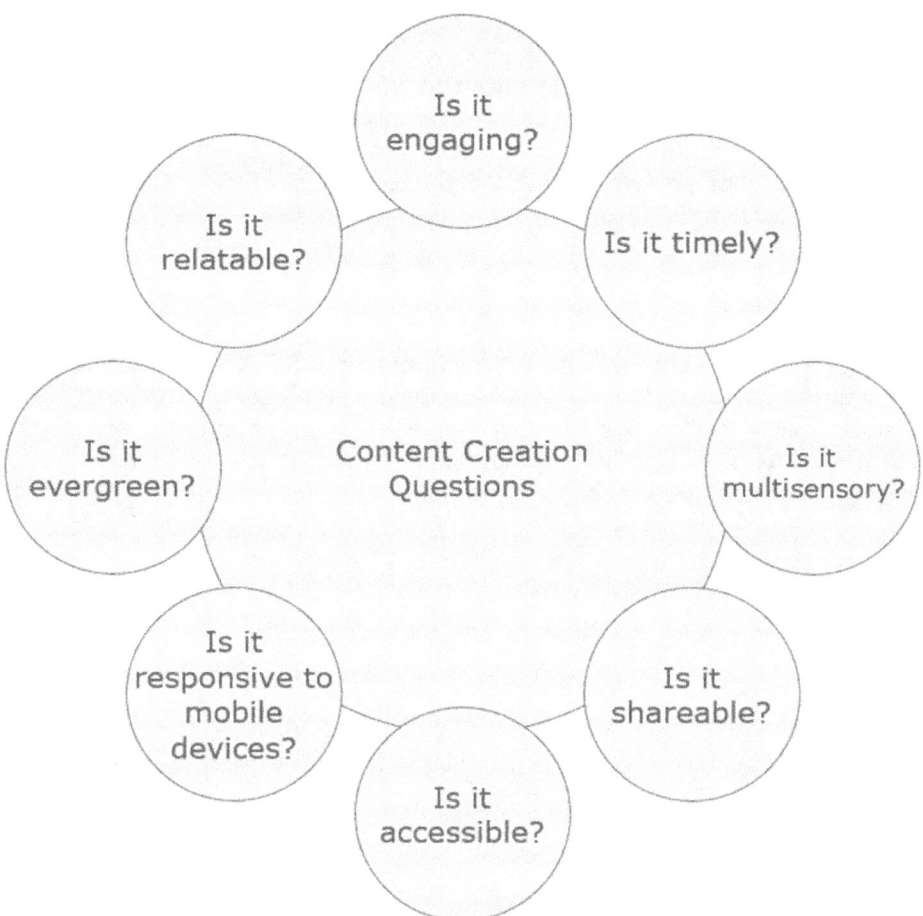

Figure 4-3. Content questions to ask when preparing content

Another goal to keep in mind is attention span. Most people do not have long attention spans. Furthermore, all learners do not have the same attention span. According to a Microsoft study, the average attention span has decreased from 12 seconds in 2000 to 8 seconds in 2018.[2] If you combine this with an online learning environment where learners can surf the Web when bored, the attention span can decrease even lower. Engaging and interactive content such as videos and Prezis can help retain attention while supplementing content. It can also motivate learners. We will discuss videos and their creation later in the book.

---

[2] www.cision.com/us/2018/01/declining-attention-killing-content-marketing-strategy/

Simplicity is often an overlooked content goal. It can be tempting to incorporate all the latest technology in your content. However, how will this benefit the learner? What value does this add to the content? If you cannot answer these questions, the technology probably is not needed. When considering any technology for content, always keep the KISS Principle in mind. You cannot go wrong with simple content because it can always be developed further.

Summary

Producing learner-centered content is important. It helps learners determine the content's value and how it can be applied to real-world situations. There is not a magic formula for creating online learning content. As long as the content centers around learners and their needs, it has a good chance of having a successful outcome.

CHAPTER 5

Learning Management Systems

In Chapter 4, you learned the basics of content creation and how both educators and learners benefit from it. Content is the heart of any learning particularly online learning. It sets the learning tone and helps learners achieve the desired course outcomes. It should focus on the quality of the content rather than the quantity. When quality content is engaging and models real-world application, learners are motivated to learn and want to learn more. Their learning experience becomes more meaningful because they see the content's value. They also can see their return on investment without the worry about the fear of missing out (FOMO).

Once content has been planned and created, it needs a storage location. Oftentimes, it is stored either on the content creator's computer or on cloud-based storages such as Google Drive, OneNote, and others. Although these are good short-term options, a more long-term, scalable solution will be needed to make the content accessible to its target audience. A learning management system (LMS) offers the solution.

© Lisa Sims 2021
L. Sims, *Effective Digital Learning*, https://doi.org/10.1007/978-1-4842-6864-3_5

Learning Management System Basics

A learning management system (LMS) is a web-based software application used to store learning content material and supporting assets for online learning. These assets can consist of

- Multimedia
- PDFs
- Images
- eBooks
- Audio files
- Social media feeds
- Videoconferencing
- RSS feeds
- Presentation files

Since LMSs are web-based, they can be accessed via a web browser from most Internet-connected devices. By accessing the LMS through a web browser, learners begin a predetermined learning path created by educators that helps them achieve the desired learning outcomes. The LMS also facilitates easy communication and sharing of information between learners and educators.

Most LMS applications offer a mobile app that can be downloaded from Apple's App Store or Android's Google Play Store. Once downloaded, educators and learners can access the course and its materials. For instance, Canvas, one of the most popular LMS platforms by Instructure and used by many postsecondary institutions, offers a mobile app that can be used to access the online classroom from anywhere. LMS platforms and their mobile apps give learners and educators the added flexibility and convenience that online learning offers. Some of the most popular paid proprietary LMSs used by larger institutions include

- Brightspace
- Blackboard Learn

LMS Considerations

Before deciding on an LMS, you must determine your budget as well as your needs. You would not go shopping for a house without a price range in mind along with a list of requirements. The same applies to shopping for an LMS. You do not want to invest in an LMS that does not meet at least 80% of your needs. This is often referred to as the Pareto Principle or the 80/20 rule named after the highly regarded economist Vilfredo Pareto.[1] Some of the questions you should ask when considering LMSs include:

- What are your goals?
- What features do you need?
- How many users can the LMS handle?
- How scalable is the LMS?
- Is the LMS within your budget?
- What type of support is offered?
- How easy is the LMS for the learners and educators to use?
- What analytics are available?
- Does the LMS provide accessibility accommodations?
- What type of security does the LMS provide?
- What is the uptime guarantee?
- Is branding available?
- What type of training is provided?
- Where is the data center located?
- What type of security does it provide?
- Is it easy to use?
- Does it have a responsive design?

Types of LMSs

When looking for an LMS solution, you will encounter many options. However, all solutions are not created the same. Unfortunately, there is not a one-size-fits-all LMS for every situation. For this reason, it is important to be clear about your needs. Most learning LMSs fall into one of three categories:

- Proprietary (commercial)
- Open source
- Free

Let us explore these types to help you select the right one based on your needs.

---

[1] www.forbes.com/sites/kevinkruse/2016/03/07/80-20-rule/#7bf759643814

Proprietary LMS

Proprietary or commercial LMS platforms are created by for-profit organizations. These LMS platforms charge a licensing fee per user which is either monthly, yearly, or subscription-based to use their systems. They are typically used by larger organizations and universities due to their expensive price tag and name reputation. Proprietary LMSs provide numerous bells and whistles features that many organizations can use now or in the future. Likewise, they typically provide hosting for the LMS as well as security. They also provide all the maintenance and software updates through a service level agreement which helps organizations that might lack technical resources. When new features become available, some form of training is typically provided to customers via webinars or recorded videos. In addition, support is provided in the form of phone, email, online chat, and online support forums which is typically included in the LMS cost. Several LMS platforms used by schools include:

- Blackboard
- Microsoft Teams
- Canvas

Although proprietary LMSs have advantages, there are also some disadvantages. For instance, customers must wait for the LMS vendor to provide software fixes and updates. Likewise, price increases are likely to occur at any time.

Open Source LMS

In addition to proprietary LMS platforms, open source LMS platforms are available. According to Opensource.com, open source software is "software with source code that anyone can inspect, modify, and enhance."[2] Compared to proprietary software, open source software does not have a licensing fee. Although freely available to download and modify, some people and organizations are still skeptical of its reliability and security compared to larger proprietary vendors such as Microsoft. Open source software can be modified, but proprietary software can only be modified by its creator. When comparing open source LMSs to proprietary LMSs, you must keep in mind that proprietary LMSs provide various levels of dedicated support within their pricing structures. This support can be provided via phone, email, online chat, or online knowledge base. Open source LMSs typically provide support through online forums and documentation. YouTube and Google searches are other ways that you can find help with your open source LMS issues. If you or organizations lack technical expertise to implement an open source LMS

---

[2]https://opensource.com/resources/what-open-source

solution, you must hire personnel or designate individuals within the organization to learn and become experts about the selected open source solution through online documentation, online forums, and trial and error. Since Apache is a popular open source web server platform maintained by the Apache Software Foundation and is used by numerous web hosts for Linux (open source) servers, you can potentially save on hosting costs compared to Windows hosting.[3] If you prefer Windows web hosting, Apache will work, but your web hosting costs might be higher. One example of an open source LMS is Moodle (Figure 5-1).

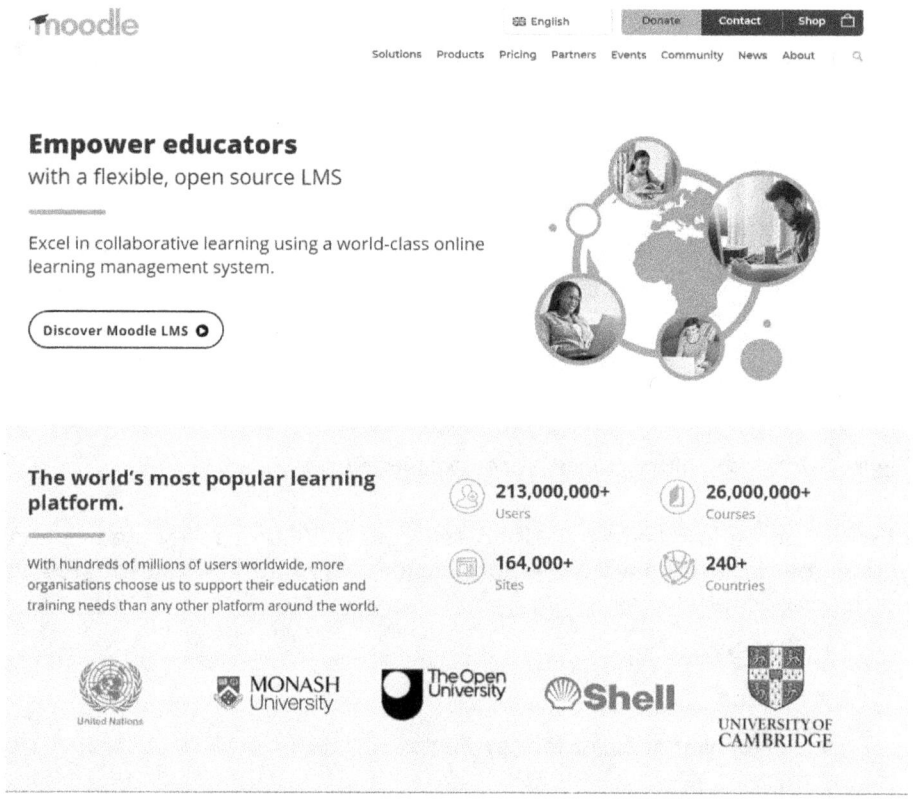

Figure 5-1. Moodle open source LMS available for download from https://moodle.org

Apache web host providers offer Moodle for free as a single-click installation from the web console called the cPanel. Some popular web hosting providers that offer Moodle include:

---

[3]www.apache.org/

Chapter 5 | Learning Management Systems

- Scala Hosting – www.scalahosting.com
- Amazon Web Services – http://Aws.amazon.com
- MoodleCloud – https://moodlecloud.com
- Lambda Solutions – www.lambdasolutions.net

Although Moodle is free, you must still pay for web hosting. Once Moodle is installed, it is easy to set up your LMS according to your course specifications. The Moodle website also provides a demo site that you can use to become more acquainted with its features[4] (Figure 5-2).

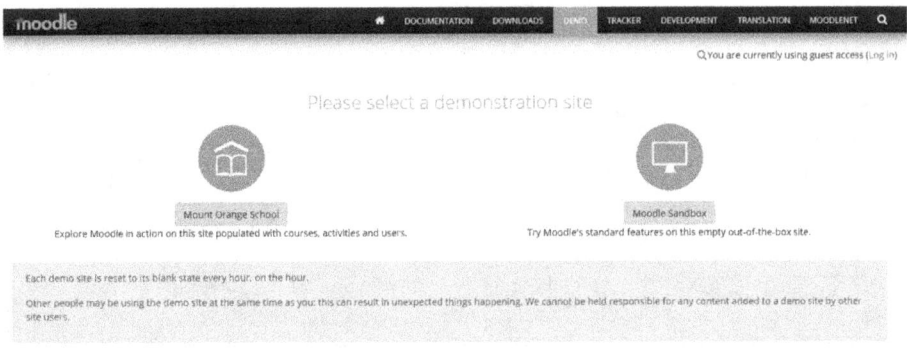

Figure 5-2. Moodle offers a demo to learn about its features

Moodle can be installed as a self-hosted option. With a self-hosted option, you or your institution will be responsible for everything involved with setting up the platform including:

- Web hosting
- Setup
- Merchant account for payments
- Maintenance
- Upgrades
- SSL certificates
- Web hosting monitoring
- Security
- Backups

---

[4]https://moodle.org/demo

- Support
- Training
- Moodle technical resource to perform maintenance and software upgrades

Initially, a self-hosted LMS solution might seem more cost-effective than a proprietary LMS, but all costs must be considered to determine the true cost of ownership. If you are not interested in a self-hosted option, Moodle offers a hosted option for a fee for small- to medium-sized businesses. With a hosted option, you pay a monthly or annual fee that provides the self-hosted options mentioned earlier along with other features. Web hosting typically starts at $100 or more per year depending on the number of users and whether shared or dedicated hosting is selected. However, you will still need a Moodle technical resource to address any technical issues and serve as a point of contact with the web host.

Free LMS Option

If an open source, self-hosted option is not an option, you might consider using Google Classroom. Google Classroom is a free hosted LMS provided by Google that can be used to facilitate interaction between educators and learners at the primary, secondary, and higher education levels (Figure 5-3). Free LMS solutions such as Google Classroom share many of the qualities of proprietary LMSs minus the price. However, depending on your intended use, you might have to pay to use an LMS such as Google Classroom.

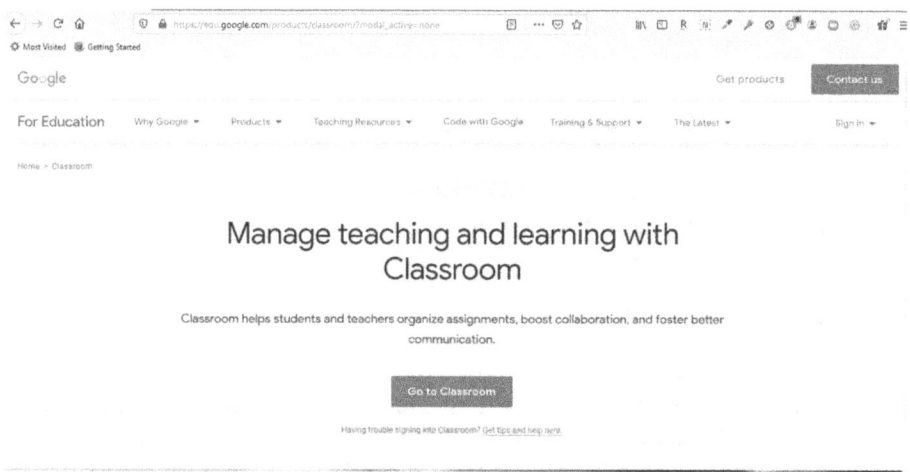

Figure 5-3. Google Classroom available as a part of Google Education Suite

Chapter 5 | Learning Management Systems

If you are planning on using Google Classroom at a school with students, G Suite for Education sign-up must be completed by your school (Figure 5-4). G Suite for Education provides the option to select the security options along with the necessary Google products to keep learners and educators information secure.

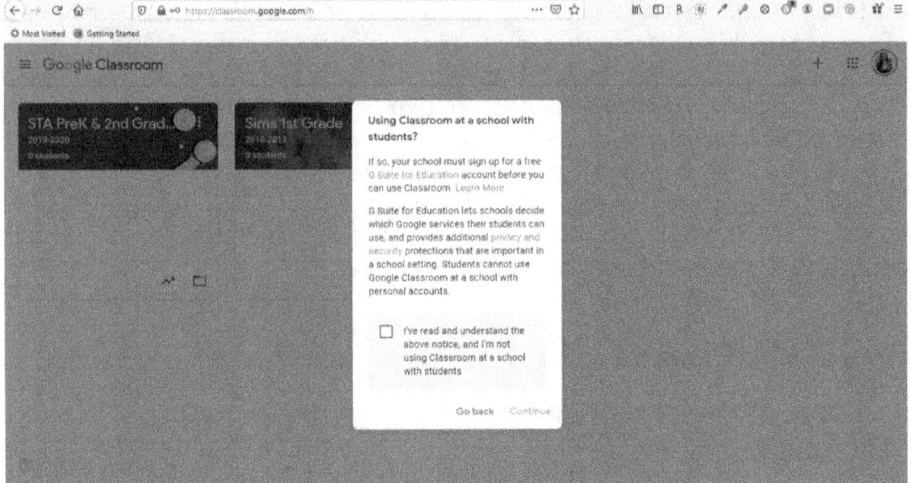

Figure 5-4. Creating a new class within Google Classroom

For users that are not members of the G Suite for Education, a Google Account is required to create a free Google Classroom. Once a Google Classroom is created, course content can be created in the following forms:

- Assignments
- Quizzes
- Video meetings via Google Meet
- Questions
- Material posted by educator
- Reuse a post
- Topic

Google Calendar, Google Drive, and the G Suite of applications such as Google Docs are also integrated within the Google Classroom to assist with course content creation. If a course requires a registration process that requires payment, you will want to review the G Suite for Education's terms of use regarding commercial purposes.

LMS Benefits

One benefit of an LMS is that all learning materials are stored in one central location in electronic format on a web server hosted outside of an organization. This is referred to as a hosted solution in which a license or subscription is purchased to use the software for a designated time. Along with this license comes training, technical support, maintenance, and upgrades to new features. The LMS is either hosted on a designated web server at a learning institution data center or at a third-party data center located in another geographical area of the world. Regardless of where the web server is located, the organization's designated administrator will have access via the Web. Although this structure typically has a lower total cost of ownership due to reduced hardware, software, infrastructure, and technology personnel costs, technical and backup personnel resources must be established. Most LMS vendors offer a guaranteed uptime along with security for the platform.

An LMS also provides analytical data about learners. Educators can review this information to track learners' activity as they progress throughout the course. It also allows you and your institution to track how much time learners are spending in the course as well as educators. Likewise, they can observe which content forms are effective and which ones might need adjustments.

Learners also benefit from using an LMS. It provides a predetermined learning path established by you to accomplish the course objectives and outcomes. The content is organized in a sequential manner, so learners acquire knowledge about one subject area before moving to the next one. Each lesson builds upon the previous one. A typical learning path can be organized either by weeks, modules, or subjects. Also, whenever new information is available, they can receive announcements from you posted in the LMS or via email. Overall, learners have immediate access to information when they need it.

LMS Limitations

The biggest limitation of many of the proprietary LMS platforms is price. Depending on the number of intended users and features, these LMS platforms can be expensive and outside of the budgets for some individuals, smaller organizations, and nonprofits. Although there are some inexpensive options available, some are not comparable to their bigger counterparts in terms of features and performance. Since most LMS platforms are software applications managed by third-party providers, they are subject to unexpected downtime and technical difficulties. To address these concerns, you can always select a larger vendor with a good reputation that provides a service level agreement guaranteeing designated uptime.

Summary

An LMS is a critical component to online learning. Although many LMSs exist, not all are created equal. Some of the most popular LMSs with extensive features can be expensive. It is imperative that you know your budget, technical resources, and requirements so that you can select the best LMS for your current and future needs. Likewise, you want to ensure that as your needs change, your LMS can easily accommodate those needs without breaking the bank and compromising performance.

CHAPTER 6

Presentation Tools

In the previous chapter, learning management systems (LMSs) were examined along with their role in helping institutions and educators organize their content. LMSs also help connect learners and educators from anywhere and any device. They also provide another communication medium while reducing paper consumption and costs. When selecting an LMS, institutions and educators must realize that there is not a one-size-fits-all LMS solution. Everyone has different needs. What works for one organization and educator might not work for another one. The primary goal of any LMS should be to help learners engage with the course content as they learn.

Content stored in LMSs can take on various forms but mostly digital. Whatever form the content is in, it serves a purpose. It also provides a benefit to the learner's learning experience. One of the most popular and common content formats is the presentation.

Choosing Your Presentation Materials

"It's not what you say but how you say it that is important." You have probably heard this adage more times than you care to remember. However, it is especially true when it comes to presentations. Presentations are a content form used to organize information about a topic. Speakers and educators

© Lisa Sims 2021
L. Sims, *Effective Digital Learning*, https://doi.org/10.1007/978-1-4842-6864-3_6

typically use them to deliver a topic's content. Presentations typically consist of slides containing bullet points of information. These bullet points are used as talking points. As the information is delivered to the audience, the audience follows along.

As you learned in Chapter 4, everyone learns according to their learning style. Most learners have a dominant or preferred learning style. This learning style helps learners not only receive information better but also understand it better. By utilizing presentations, educators are able to address not only visual learners but also auditory learners. Presentation slides, also called slide decks, can utilize different color schemes to elicit certain emotions in learners. Similar to the psychology of color subconsciously used in marketing campaigns, educators can apply the same effect. Websites such as Adobe Color (https://color.adobe.com) and www.presentationteam.com can assist you in selecting the right color scheme for your presentation. As you are creating your presentation, do not forget about branding and include your organization's logo on each slide in the header or footer area.

Presentations can be designed to be aesthetically appealing to keep learners engaged. For instance, many presentation software applications provide templates that can be used to create content rather than starting from scratch. Some of the content that can be included within presentations to engage learners includes:

- Images
- Charts
- Animations
- Music
- Shapes
- Multimedia
- Transitions

Without presentations, learners would rely solely on their auditory learning style which might not be their preferred learning style. We all can recall our college days when we had a professor who lectured for the entire class period without a presentation. In an online learning environment, it can be difficult for learners to watch a talking head video delivering a presentation and remain engaged. It is easy to miss information that is heard rather than seen.

Presentation Creation Strategies

When most people hear the words "online presentation," PowerPoint immediately comes to their minds. The next thing that comes to mind is the term "Death By PowerPoint." The term "Death By PowerPoint" has been attributed to Angela R. Garber, but many people had already experienced it although did not name it.[1] In a general sense, it refers to the boring effect caused by a PowerPoint presentation and its presenter. Many effects can be added to presentations to make them interesting. However, all of them are not needed. Although presentation tools allow you to create presentations any way you want, it is good to follow some industry best practices to achieve a maximum impact. Your content and its impact on learners should be the primary focus rather than how many of the presentation software's features you can implement.

KISS Principle

With so many features at your disposal, you might want to include all of them in your presentation. However, this is not a good idea. You will not only overwhelm your students but also lose your message at the same time. Whenever you have to design a presentation, you should always keep the KISS principle in mind. The KISS principle, short for Keep It Simple Silly, implies that you should keep your presentation and its components as simple as possible. For instance, TED Talks are simple and straightforward. The focus is on delivering quality content rather than fancy presentation slides. Some ways to incorporate the KISS principle in your presentation include:

- Use two to three fonts for consistency
- Include enough white space to improve readability
- Apply two to three color schemes consistently throughout slides
- Use bullets for better readability

Reducing Clutter

Some PowerPoint slides contain too much information such as text and images. Learners perceive them as being busy, overwhelming, and difficult to read. An unfortunate result is that learners zone out and are no longer engaged. Learners have short attention spans, and your presentation must

---

[1] www.free-power-point-templates.com/articles/death-by-powerpoint/#:~:text=To%20make%20it%20simple%2C%20Death%20by%20PowerPoint%20refers,applications%20to%20highlight%20a%20horrible%20presentation%20in%20general

grab and keep it until the end. A slide is not meant to contain everything about your topic. It should only highlight your topic's key points. This not only applies to text on the slides but also images and bullets. Always remember, less is more.

Limit Animations

Recall the last time you watched a presentation that contained animations. How did you feel when you saw the first animation? As the presentation continued, more animations were used. How did you feel? Annoyed? How do you think your students would feel? When used sparingly, animations can spice up a presentation. However, too many animations can become distracting and appear amateurish. Limit your animations to no more than one or two in a presentation.

Limit Transitions

Transitions between slides can be a nice effect. As with animations, too much of anything can quickly become a bad thing. With transitions, you want to make sure they are consistent and do not distract from your presentation. If you choose to use transitions, consider using one or two consistently throughout your presentation.

Use Quality Images

In addition to selecting a good color scheme and design for your presentation, quality images are a necessity. Poor quality images can distract from your presentation's message. Your images need to be able to stand alone to support your topic. They also need to be professional and high resolution which can be scaled up or down without affecting the image quality. Likewise, make sure you have copyright permission to use images outside of PowerPoint or any other presentation tool you use. They should also be used sparingly on a slide. One or two images per slide is a good practice. Otherwise, your slide can quickly become cluttered. In Chapter 11, you will learn about some free resources for locating images. Other resources for locating paid, high-resolution royalty-free images include:

- Getty Images – www.gettyimages.com
- Shutterstock – www.shutterstock.com
- Dreamstime – www.dreamstime.com

Effective Digital Learning

Use Music Sparingly

Everyone likes music. Music connects and energizes us. Using music in your presentation can be good, but you must know where to use it. For instance, it is not a good idea to use music throughout your presentation. However, it can be used at the beginning of your presentation to set the tone for your presentation. You must also select the right type of music for your audience to produce the right effect. For example, you would not want to open your presentation with a slow musical selection for a young children's audience. Children are full of energy so a more upbeat song would be better. When selecting music to add to your presentation, make sure that it is royalty-free to avoid copyright issues. Royalty-free music allows you to pay for it once but use it an unlimited number of times. Some common sources of royalty-free music include:

- Premiumbeat.com
- Bensound.com
- Youtube.com

Presentation Tool Options

Still feel uneasy about creating an engaging presentation? No problem. The good news is that there are many presentation software applications available to help educators create their presentations for maximum engagement and learner impact. Before creating your presentation, it is a good idea to brainstorm your presentation ideas. Likewise, if you are not experienced with creating presentations, look around for inspiration. Some good websites to help you find inspiration include:

- Slideshare.net
- www.free-power-point-templates.com
- https://powerpointify.com
- Powerhouse.net

Microsoft PowerPoint

For years, Microsoft PowerPoint has been the industry standard and leader for creating PowerPoint presentations. Currently, it is available with Microsoft 365. It also has a free app available in Apple's App Store and Android's Google Play Store. To check educator and learner eligibility to receive Microsoft Office 365 for free, visit www.microsoft.com/en-us/education/products/office (Figure 6-1). If you are not an educator or student, you can either use the free apps or purchase Office 365 from the Microsoft website.

Chapter 6 | Presentation Tools

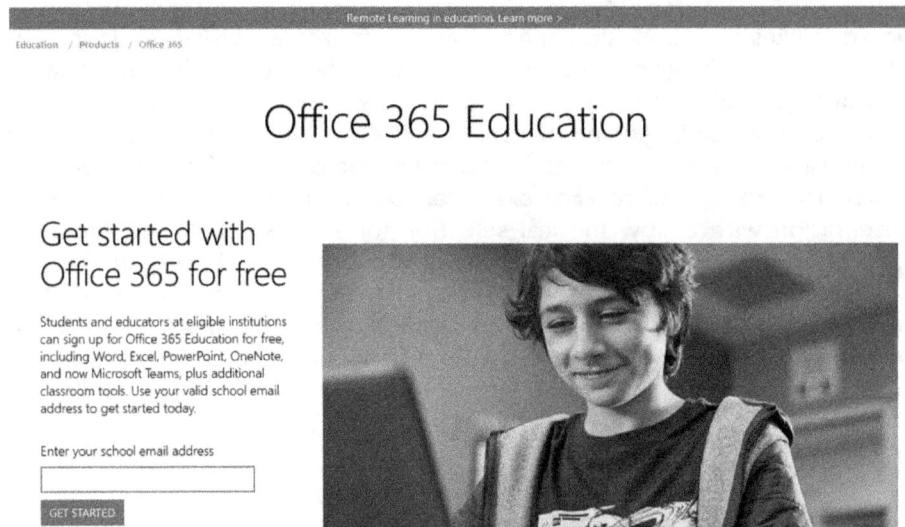

Figure 6-1. Check your eligibility for Office 365 for free

Creating a presentation can be a daunting task, but PowerPoint provides presentation templates to get you started (Figure 6-2). These templates are available on the Microsoft Office website. Not only does PowerPoint create impressive presentations but also create videos. You will learn more about this in an upcoming chapter.

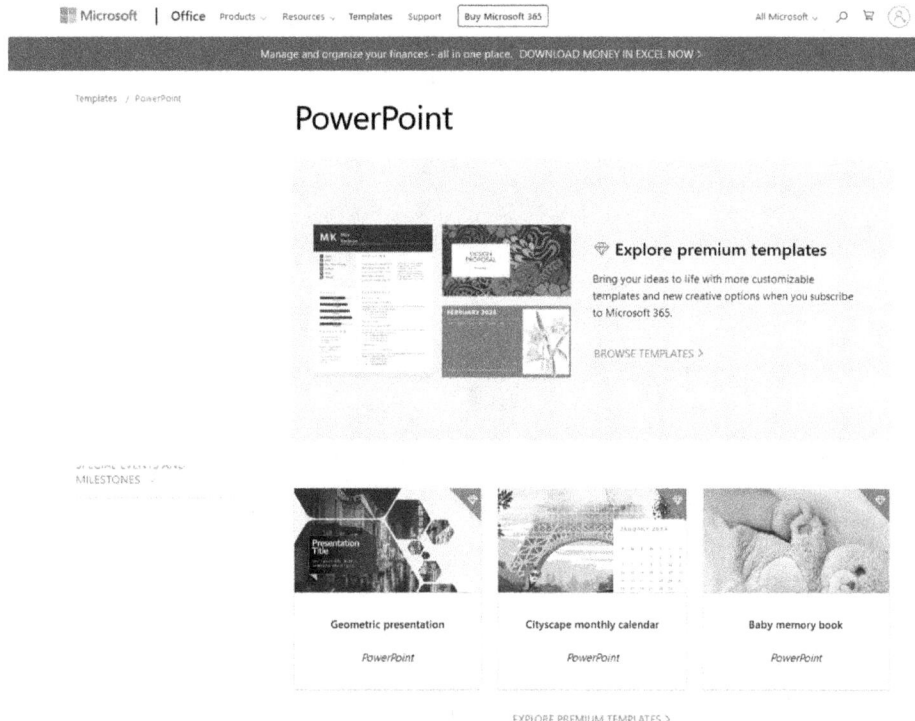

Figure 6-2. Microsoft Office website for PowerPoint templates

Prezi

Prezi is a type of presentation that allows you to create interactive presentations as well as videos (Figure 6-3).

Chapter 6 | Presentation Tools

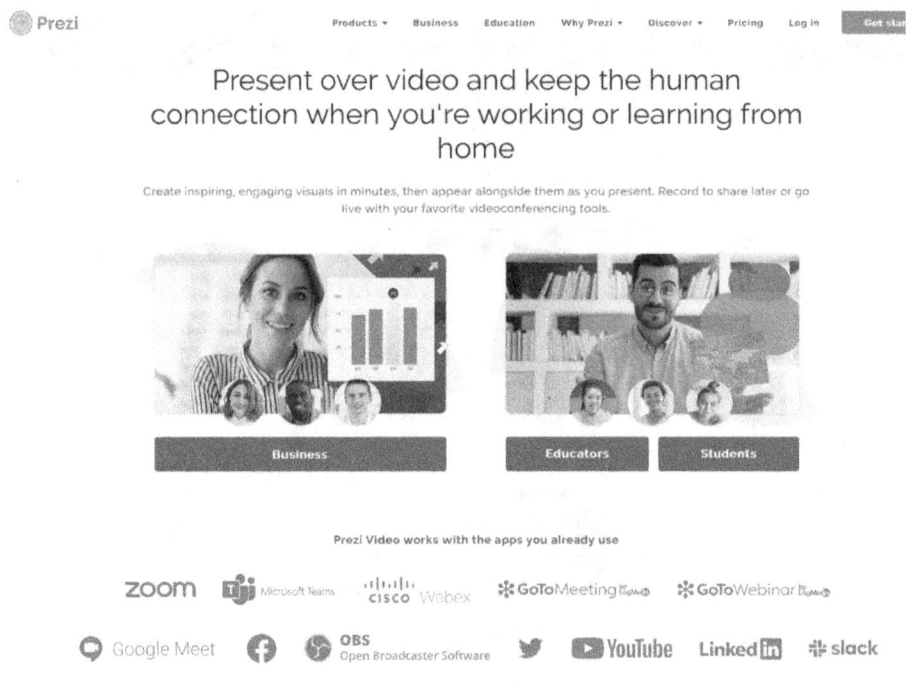

Figure 6-3. Sign up for a Prezi account at https://prezi.com/

Prezi gives you the ability to interact with your presentation content on screen. In other words, it brings your presentation to life in front of your students. It is a great way to keep students engaged. There are three Prezi products that you can use to create interactive content:

- Prezi Presents for presentations
- Prezi Video for videos
- Prezi Design

Prezi presentations can be used within Google Classroom, Zoom, Microsoft Teams, and other webinar platforms. Likewise, PowerPoint presentations can be imported into Prezi, but it is more difficult to export a Prezi to PowerPoint.

Google Slides

A free alternative to Microsoft PowerPoint is Google Slides. Google Slides can be used for personal and business use (a part of Google Suite for businesses) to create presentations. It is available on Windows, Apple computers, and Google Chromebooks and tablets and has a mobile app for Apple and Android mobile devices (Figure 6-4). To begin using Google Slides, you must have a Google Account which is free to create.

Effective Digital Learning

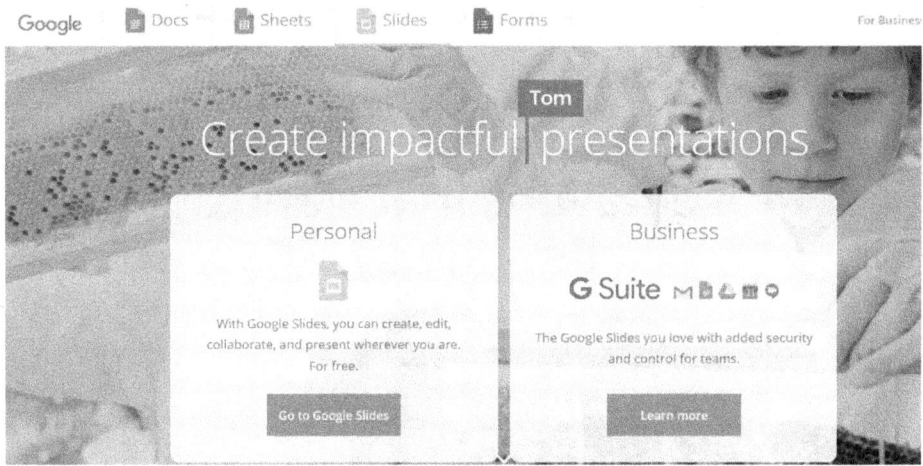

Figure 6-4. Google Slides available from www.google.com/slides

If you are familiar with Microsoft PowerPoint, you will have no problem adjusting to using Google Slides. The process of creating your presentations is the same as creating presentations within PowerPoint.

Apple Keynote

For Apple Mac and mobile users, the Keynote application is another presentation option (Figure 6-5). It can be installed for free via the App Store.

Chapter 6 | Presentation Tools

Figure 6-5. Apple's Keynote can be downloaded from www.apple.com/keynote/ or the Apple App Store

Unfortunately, if you have an older Apple Mac, you might be required to pay a one-time fee. Once you complete your presentation, it can be exported in one of the following formats:

- PDF
- PowerPoint
- Movie
- Animated GIF
- Images
- Keynote Theme

Similar to PowerPoint, Keynote offers plenty of templates to get started. It also works with Apple Pencil on iPads to allow for drawings and illustrations.

LibreOffice Impress

Another presentation software application is LibreOffice Impress (Figure 6-6). LibreOffice Impress is packaged with the free LibreOffice suite. LibreOffice replaced OpenOffice.org and has been a solution for millions of users who could not afford or did not want to pay for Microsoft Office. Similar to Microsoft Office, LibreOffice has an extension library that contains templates to aid in your presentation design. Once you complete your presentation, it can be saved in many different formats including PowerPoint, PDF, and others.

Figure 6-6. LibreOffice Impress presentation available for download from www.libreoffice.org

Summary

It does not matter what presentation software application you use. You must use what works with not only the devices you have available but also allows you to present your content in the best way possible to engage learners. Each presentation application allows you to be as creative as you like. It is up to you to think outside of the box.

CHAPTER 7

Webinars

Presenting subject matter to learners in an interesting way that ignites engagement is the essence of teaching. It is especially important in online learning. As discussed in Chapter 6, presentations are used by educators to explain a particular subject matter topic to learners while being aesthetically appealing. They also not only organize content into digestible chunks but also guide the learner along a predetermined learning path. With numerous presentation application options available for free and a fee, educators can deliver their content in new and refreshing ways.

In the age of Covid-19, presentations are typically paired with webinars. In online learning environments, it is easy for learners to sometimes feel like they are the only ones on a deserted island. Although there can be communication and collaboration between learners and educators, they still need to feel connected to the educator beyond seeing the educator's profile picture or viewing his or her biography. In some instances, educators pre-record a "talking head" video that only shows them from the waist up delivering content. As an educator, you need another medium to connect with learners. This is where webinars come into play in the online learning environment and can help bridge the gap.

© Lisa Sims 2021
L. Sims, *Effective Digital Learning*, https://doi.org/10.1007/978-1-4842-6864-3_7

The New Meeting Place

According to webopedia.com, a webinar, short for web-based seminar, can be defined as "a presentation, lecture, workshop or seminar that is transmitted over the web using *video conferencing software*."[1] During the Covid-19 pandemic, webinars have quickly become the preferred way for many to safely meet while practicing social distancing. Although many organizations were already using webinars prior to the pandemic, many that were hesitant jumped on the webinar bandwagon. As a result, webinar usage soared. Organizations began using webinars to stay connected with remote employees. Educators began using webinars to connect with learners and deliver course content.

Webinar Advantages

Webinars do not require people to be physically present in the same physical room or location. As long as people have a fast Internet connection, they can attend webinars while being geographically located anywhere in the world. In online learning, webinars can be considered the modern-day college lecture hall or auditorium from traditional learning. Compared to traditional lecture halls or auditoriums, seating is virtual, and attendance is sometimes optional. Webinars occur at designated times. If learners miss a live scheduled webinar, recordings are often made available that can be watched at a more convenient time. In traditional learning, learners would not have this option. In addition to lectures, workshops, and seminars, you can use webinars to enhance learning by providing the following:

- Office hours
- Group discussions
- Brainstorming sessions
- Staff meetings
- Team projects

Many webinar platforms provide accessibility options such as closed captions for learners that might need it. Webinars are an effective way to engage learners with customized content. However, there are some limitations. For instance, many free webinar platforms limit the webinar duration along with the number of attendees. It can also be difficult to keep learners engaged.

---

[1] www.webopedia.com/TERM/W/Webinar.html

Webinar Requirements

Most in-person functions can be modified and conducted via a webinar. Technology advances have made it relatively easy and cost-effective to conduct or participate in webinars from any Internet-connected device. Most laptops and mobile devices already come equipped with cameras and built-in microphones that can be used during a webinar. To ensure good quality video and audio, you might want to use a high-definition (HD) webcam and a lapel microphone. However, one of the main webinar requirements is a fast Internet connection. Without a fast Internet connection, you and your learners can experience delays in video and audio quality which can interfere with the learning experience. Since most webinars occur within a web browser or a webinar platform's mobile app, educators and learners can participate from any Internet-connected device and from any location. All you would need to do is invite your students to the webinar via email via webinar platform or post an announcement in your LMS with the webinar link. Lastly, a clean and well-lighted background is essential. Many webinar platforms such as Zoom provide virtual background options that can help present a more professional webinar experience.

Webinar Delivery Strategies

Like the traditional in-person learning model, webinar platforms provide a medium for teachers and students to see each other in real time in the online learning environment. They also help to maintain some form of socialization. However, many educators struggle with effectively using webinars and their tools to present their materials and engage with their students. Webinar tools allow for more engagement than simply lecturing to your students with presentation slides. To maximize your students' learning experience, it is important to familiarize yourself with the features of your selected webinar platform. For instance, YouTube is a good starting point to gain tips and tricks on using a selected webinar platform. Your students consider you the expert. By not being prepared, you do not want to appear as a novice. Students will quickly tell and become disengaged. To prevent this from occurring, there are some strategies you can use to prepare.

Style and Tone

Before you conduct your first webinar, it is important to determine your webinar style. Your webinar style will greatly influence your students' level of engagement. Will it be a lecture with PowerPoints or more open discussion? What will be your tone? Will it be authoritarian, conversational, or entertaining? Many educators have started modelling their webinars after

TED Talks.[2] TED Talks rely heavily on a presenter's message rather than PowerPoint slides. Images are often used to support points rather than PowerPoint slides filled with text and bullet points. The presenter must use tools such as storytelling, humor, voice, body language, and others to keep the viewers engaged. Reviewing several TED Talks is a good idea to see if this style will work for you and your students. Some other alternatives to follow for inspiration include:

- The Moth – themoth.org
- Ignite – ignitetalks.io
- 99U – 99u.adobe.com
- Talks at Google – talksat.withgoogle.com
- Big Think – bigthink.com

Polls

Everyone loves polls. Students are no different. Webinar platforms such as Zoom provide the ability to create polls that can be displayed during webinars. However, this functionality is only available for paid accounts. Polls can keep your students engaged during the meeting or webinar. For example, before your meeting or webinar begins, you can create simple polls in the Zoom portal meeting management that can be displayed to students to cast their votes on various course topics. Once everyone has voted, you can reveal the results. Based on the poll's results, you and your students can participate in interesting discussions.

Whiteboards

Most webinar platforms provide a whiteboard feature that resembles those found in traditional in-person classrooms. In an online environment, a whiteboard can be used to illustrate difficult concepts. For instance, you could use the whiteboard to show students how to solve a math problem. You could also diagram a process to make it easier for students to understand. It can also be used for brainstorming ideas. Like traditional learning, you could call on a student and allow them to provide the answer on the whiteboard. All of this helps to increase student engagement and positive course outcomes.

---

[2] www.ted.com

Breakout Rooms

In traditional learning, teachers can divide students into groups for group work. Group work supports students not only to work together but also be open to others' points of view. The same concept can be applied within a webinar. For instance, Zoom allows you to either manually or automatically assign students to groups referred to as breakout rooms. Zoom participants can also choose to join a breakout room. These breakout rooms can be created when scheduling a meeting or during the meeting. While in these breakout rooms, they can collaborate on their assignment while you monitor each of the breakout rooms. Once their time is up, you can bring everyone back to the main webinar together for discussion. Breakout rooms can provide opportunities for socialization and interaction that many students and teachers need in a virtual environment. However, in Zoom, breakout rooms are only available for paid plans. Microsoft Teams offers a similar concept.

Questions and Answers (Q&A)

Students like to ask questions, so why not let them? Within your webinar, you can allow students to do so. Many webinar platforms such as Zoom provide a raise hand button that students can click to let you know that they have a question. Once you acknowledge them, you can either ask them to hold the question until the end of the webinar or unmute one student's microphone at a time to speak. You can also encourage students to type their questions in the chatroom. However, you want to make sure that you are monitoring the chat so you do not miss any questions that might arise.

Videos

Sharing a video about your course material in your webinar is another way to connect with students and keep them engaged. You can share a video from your computer or YouTube to help students understand the course material. Be careful not to select a long video. Remember that your students have short attention spans, so keep the video under 2 minutes. You also want to make sure that the video is engaging and provides closed captioning. Since your Internet speed affects the video's playback speed, it is a good practice to test your Internet connection speed with www.speedtest.org before any online meeting and webinar.

Gamification

Regardless of age, everyone loves games. Remember the Angry Birds and Candy Crush craze? Games are fun and relieve stress. They are also educational. Why not keep your students engaged by incorporating games that supplement your lesson into your webinar? You can create games such as Family Feud or Jeopardy by using PowerPoint templates available on the Web. You can also find free games online that can be used during your webinar session. Once you select your games, you can assign your students to teams or have your students play against other students online. Likewise, you can also include digital badges with tools such as www.accredible.com to celebrate your student's success. Some good sources for online games include

- Quizlet.com
- Quizzizz.com
- American Museum of Natural History – www.amnh.org/explore/ology/games

Livestreaming

When was the last time you watched a Facebook Live event that was recorded with Zoom or another webinar platform? Livestreaming is available on the following social media platforms:

- Facebook
- LinkedIn
- Periscope
- Instagram

Over the past few years, livestreaming has become increasingly popular. What is livestreaming? Livestreaming provides anyone the ability to broadcast their video message using the Internet. Social media platforms such as Facebook, LinkedIn, Instagram, and others provide a free option. Livestreaming also saves time by allowing you to reach a wider audience on social media platforms who might not have registered for your webinar.

Webinars can be simultaneously broadcast to multiple social media platforms with the help of livestreaming software. Livestreaming software is available to allow you to livestream your webinars to various social media platforms simultaneously. Prior to livestreaming, you must have social media accounts on your targeted platforms. You also must have your RTMP URL and stream key that are available from your social media platforms. The stream key is generated by each of your social media accounts and is provided to your livestream software for simultaneous broadcasts. Some popular livestream programs include

- Restream Studio
- Castr.io
- OBS Studio
- StreamYard

Before using livestreaming software with your webinars, you should decide which social media platforms you will target. Next, you also need to have a computer with a fast processor (i5 or higher) and ample memory (8GB or more) to handle the livestreaming needs. A fast Internet is also a requirement. Likewise, it is a good idea to practice your webinar delivery to correct any issues so that it appears polished.

Webinar Platform Options

Now that you know how you can make your webinars engaging, it is time to select a webinar platform. Many free and paid webinar platforms are available that share some of the core functionality along with providing different features. Let's review a few.

Zoom

Since the Covid-19 pandemic forced closures of schools, businesses, churches, and other businesses, Zoom usage has skyrocketed. At the time of this writing, Zoom offers a free account that will allow up to 100 participants for either a 40-minute time period for three or more participants or unlimited one-to-one meetings (Figure 7-1). It can be used either within a web browser or via their Zoom app which is available in the Apple App Store or Google Play Store.

Chapter 7 | Webinars

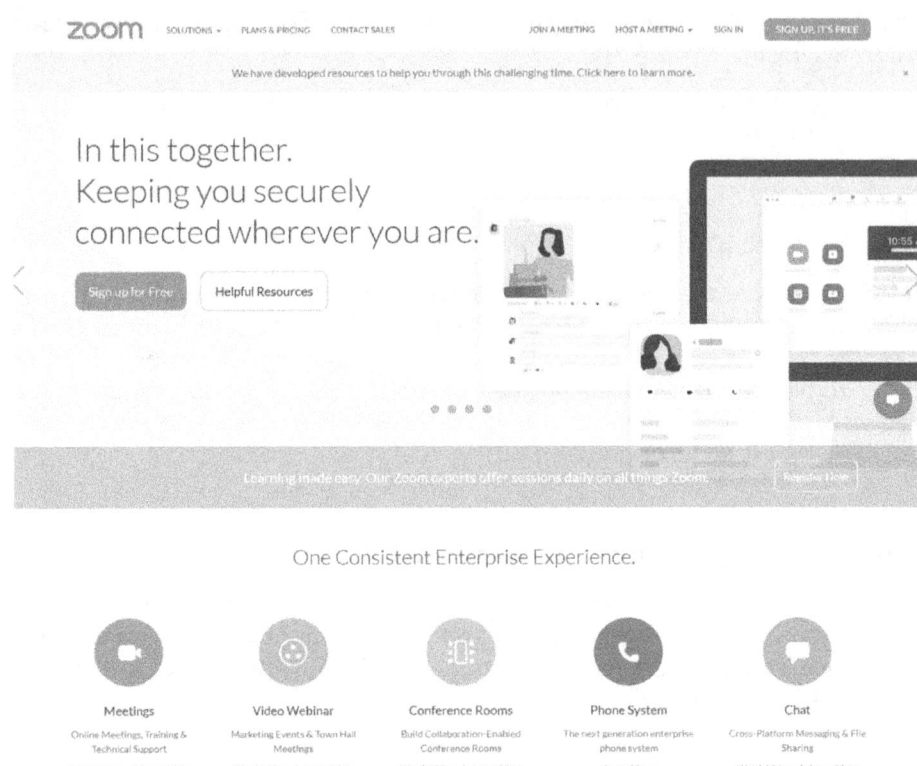

Figure 7-1. Zoom platform available from www.zoom.us

Most educators and learners are already familiar with Zoom. It is easy to use. For those unfamiliar with it, it does not have a steep learning curve. However, security has been an area of concern. During the Covid-19 pandemic, Zoombombing has become a new normal. According to howtogeek.com, Zoombombing is "when an uninvited person joins a Zoom meeting in an attempt to gain a few cheap laughs at the expense of the participants by providing inappropriate content or comments".[3] As a result of Zoombombing, Zoom has increased its security and suggests that meeting hosts perform the following:

- Provide passwords for meetings
- Enable the waiting room to verify and approve registered users
- Lock the meeting once all attendees arrive
- Mute participants' microphones upon arrival
- Lock attendee's ability to share their screen

---

[3] www.howtogeek.com/667183/what-is-zoombombing-and-how-can-you-stop-it/

Zoom offers apps that can be installed to make functions such as collaboration, analytics, scheduling, and others easier to accomplish within Zoom meetings, webinars, and breakout rooms. To install the apps, you would need to sign into your Zoom account via zoom.us. Some of the Zoom App Marketplace apps include

- Analytics
- CRM
- Collaboration
- Customer service
- Education
- Event management

Zoom also provides the ability to have virtual backgrounds. A virtual background replaces your background that is visible to learners via your web camera with a computer-generated one you select. It gives your meeting or webinar a professional look and hides a cluttered background. To enable virtual backgrounds, navigate to Settings ➤ In Meeting (Advanced) option in your Zoom web portal and enable the virtual backgrounds option. To browse available virtual backgrounds in your Zoom account, click the Resources link and click the virtual background link. Virtual backgrounds can be purchased online or created with tools such as Canva.com.

Microsoft Teams

Another webinar solution is Microsoft Teams. Microsoft Teams, part of Microsoft 365, offers both free and paid plans (Figure 7-2). You can use any of the Microsoft Office apps within Microsoft Teams for collaboration as well as during meetings. It can also be used within a web browser, desktop app, or mobile app from either Apple's App Store or Google's Play Store. It supports Google Chrome, Firefox, and Microsoft Edge browsers. At the time of this writing and in response to Covid-19, there is no limit on meeting time and size.

Chapter 7 | Webinars

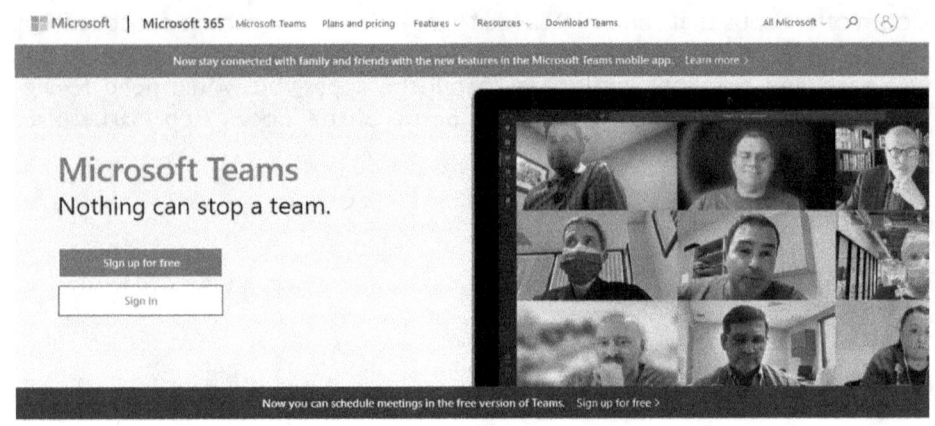

Figure 7-2. Microsoft Teams for online collaboration and more

With Microsoft Teams, everything revolves around a team concept. Before you can schedule a meeting, you must create a team. Once your team is created, you can assign members and invite them to online meetings with audio and video. Microsoft Teams also provides real-time captions based on what is being said in a meeting which is helpful for learners with accessibility needs. However, those captions are not saved once the meeting has ended. Since it is part of Microsoft 365, it offers security to protect your meetings and its materials from potential Zoombombing as experienced in Zoom.

AnyMeeting

Another available webinar option is AnyMeeting. It is a videoconferencing software that is available via a web browser (www.anymeeting.com) or through their app in Apple's App Store or Google Play Store. At the time of this writing, it is free until December 31, 2020, with no meeting time limits (Figure 7-3) and allows access to all pro features. Similar to the other webinar software mentioned, AnyMeeting offers the same functionality.

Effective Digital Learning

Figure 7-3. AnyMeeting videoconferencing software available from www.anymeeting.com

Google Meet

Previously called Google Hangouts, Google Meet is another option. It is operated by Google and requires a Google Account. Like the other options, it offers free and paid plans (Figure 7-4). It also can be used within a web browser, through Gmail, or via its app that can be downloaded from the Apple Play Store or Google Play Store. At the time of this writing, a free account can have a meeting with 100 participants for 60 minutes. Organizations and schools have increased participants along with meeting time but must have a G Suite account.

Chapter 7 | Webinars

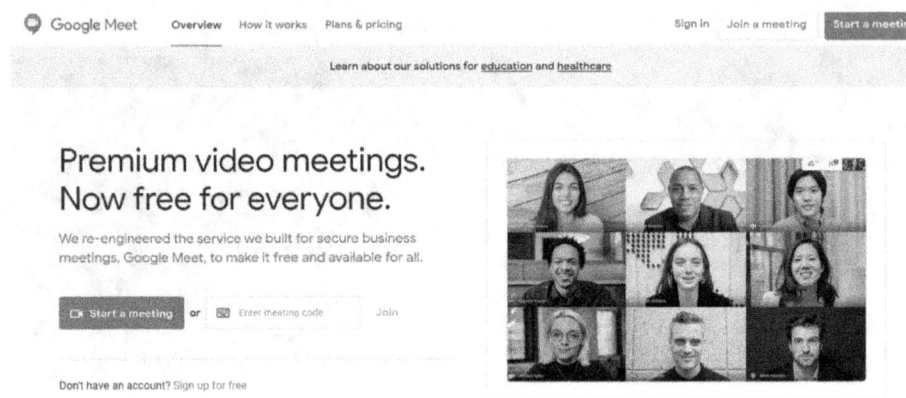

Figure 7-4. Google Meet available for use at apps.google.com/meet

Summary

Webinars are an effective method of bringing a personal touch to an online learning environment. They allow you to connect with learners all over the world using the Internet. As you have seen, there are many options to choose from. However, there is no right or wrong webinar software solution. It all depends on the number of learners, the time limit, budget, and your purpose as to which solution will work best for you.

CHAPTER 8

Podcasts

In Chapter 7, you learned about webinars and their impact in delivering content while fostering engagement within an online learning environment. Webinars are an effective tool in online learning to create a personalized connection between educators and learners similar to what is available in traditional learning. With many free and paid options available for computers and mobile devices, webinars are within reach of anyone who desires to use them.

Learner engagement is a critical component to the online learning experience. No two learners learn the same. With many different and affordable content options available today than in the past, educators have more tools at their disposal to help with engagement. With more learners utilizing mobile and wearable devices than ever before, educators need more flexible solutions. One of those solutions is podcasts.

Podcast Basics

Podcasts have been around for a long time. According to howstuffworks.com, in 2004, podcasts were originally created by former MTV video jockey, Adam Curry, and software developer, Dave Winer, after Curry wrote a program called iPodder to download Internet radio broadcasts to his iPod.[1] Other developers enhanced his code and podcasting as we know it skyrocketed.

---

[1]https://computer.howstuffworks.com/internet/basics/podcasting.htm#pt1

© Lisa Sims 2021
L. Sims, *Effective Digital Learning*, https://doi.org/10.1007/978-1-4842-6864-3_8

Chapter 8 | Podcasts

Based on its name, many people incorrectly associated podcasts only with Apple's iPod devices. However, most people commonly use many different mobile devices to listen to podcasts because they are portable and can be listened to on the go. For example, Apple's Podcasts app can be used to listen to podcasts on iOS devices (Figure 8-1). Previously on iOS devices, podcasts were included within the iTunes app. On Android devices, podcasts are available from the Google Podcasts app (Figure 8-2).

Figure 8-1. Apple's Podcasts app available on iOS devices

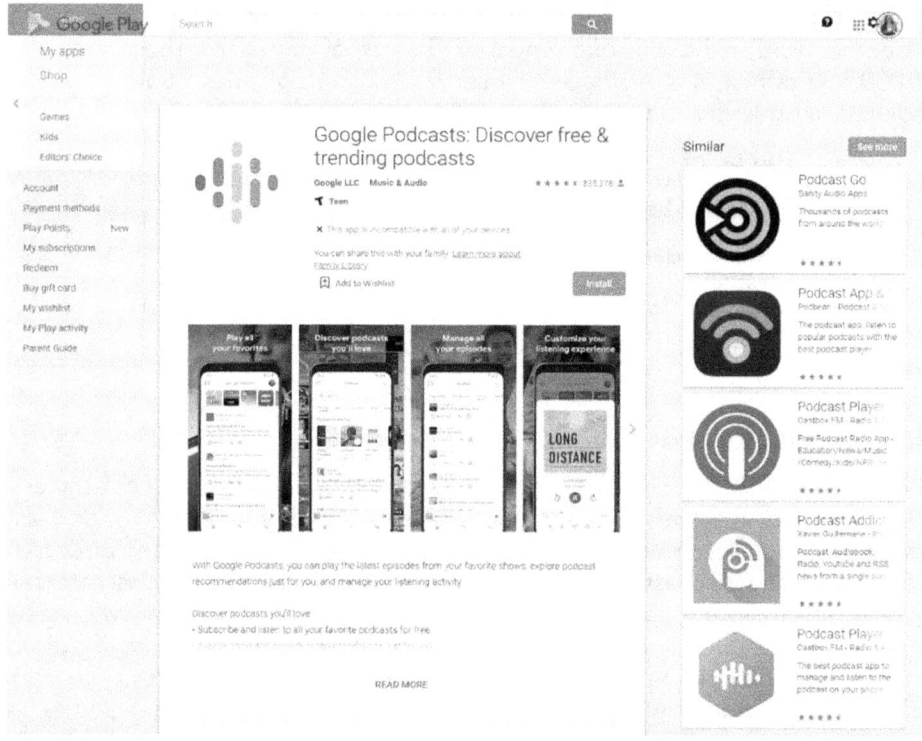

Figure 8-2. Google Podcasts app available in Google Play Store for Android devices to locate and listen to podcasts

Other podcast apps available on both iOS and Android devices include

- Pandora
- Spotify
- Amazon Music
- Stitcher
- Deezer
- TuneIn

Podcasts are a series of audio files called episodes with content tailored to a podcast's theme. The files are available on demand from podcast directories online or from any mobile device. Most podcast episode lengths range from 30 minutes to 1 hour. Typically, a podcast format follows that of a radio talk show where a host conducts an entire episode or invites guests. Every podcast has a file associated with it called really simple syndication (RSS). The RSS feed provides podcast information to programs called RSS readers along with podcast directories so that potential subscribers can discover and listen to podcasts. Podcasthosting.org reported that as of July 2020, there are over 1,000,000 podcasts available with over 29 million episodes.[2] Some popular education podcasts today include:

- The Google Teacher Tribe
- The Book Love Foundation
- Flipped Learning Worldwide
- House of #EdTech
- The 10 Minute Teacher

Podcast Advantages

Podcasts are good tools to use in traditional and online learning. For starters, podcasts are currently available on any subject. If you visit any podcast directory and search on a particular topic, you will find numerous podcasts. With so many podcasts already available, you do not have to recreate the wheel which saves you time and effort. Next, you always know when new content is available. Once you subscribe to a podcast, you receive notifications via your podcast app when new episodes are released which saves time from checking the podcast directory for new content. Since they are free and easily available in podcast directories on the Web, you will never run out of invaluable learning resources.

To include podcasts within your online learning environment, you would need either the podcast's RSS feed or the podcast episode URL which can be found on the Web. Once you have these, you can either send out weekly announcements to learners from your learning management system, include in weekly lectures, or send emails notifying students of the podcast or podcast episode. Most learning management systems allow RSS feeds to be easily inserted within announcements that are sent to learners within the LMS or via email.

You also can start a discussion post in your learning management system and include the podcast episode URL to not only supplement your course material but also spark discussion. Furthermore, you can create assignments based on a podcast episode URL shared with learners that reinforces the lesson. Since learners are always on their mobile devices, students can benefit from podcasts flexibility and portability of being available via the Web or apps on mobile or wearable devices to enhance not only the course content but also their learning experience.

---

[2]https://podcasthosting.org/podcast-statistics/?gclid=EAIaIQobChMIt6zArP vw6gIVWwiICR1xUASCEAAYASAAEgJpePD_BwE

Although most podcasts are audio, they can also include video which will further supplement learners' understanding of the material. As we discussed in Chapter 4, video podcasts can be another way to support audio and visual learners. Video podcasts are saved in the .mp4 format as opposed to .mp3 which is strictly audio. During the Covid-19 pandemic and social distancing, video podcasts can easily be recorded remotely with free tools such as:

- Zoom
- Microsoft Teams
- iMovie Maker
- OBS Studio

Once your video podcast episode has been recorded in .mp4 format, it can easily be shared on YouTube, social media platforms, and blogs for great visibility and promotion.

Podcast Planning

You do not have to depend on others to create podcast episodes for your online learning needs. You can inexpensively and easily do so yourself. If you decide to create your own podcast, you need to do some initial planning. This planning will consist of answering some basic questions about your podcast:

- What will be the theme or topic of my podcast?
- Will it be an audio or video podcast or combination?
- What will be the duration of a podcast episode?
- How often will podcast episodes be released?
- How will you promote your podcast?
- Will you solely conduct the podcast episode or invite guests?
- Will you have an introduction with or without music?
- What will your podcast image look like?
- How will you end your show?
- How will you structure your podcast episodes?

Podcast Creation Equipment

For beginners, an audio podcast is the fastest and cheapest way to begin because you probably already own the necessary items. For the items that you do not have, many are available for free or inexpensively.

Microphones

At the heart of any good podcast is the sound quality. To have good sound quality, you need a quality microphone. A good, quality microphone will improve the quality of the recording. To be taken as a professional, you want to provide your potential subscribers with not only quality content but also quality sound. An inexpensive quality microphone for podcasting can be purchased for around $100. The Blue Yeti is a good beginning podcasters microphone with good quality sound that is used by podcasters (Figure 8-3).

Figure 8-3. The Blue Yeti microphone is a good choice for podcast beginners

As your podcast needs changes, you can always upgrade to a premium microphone such as the Heil Sound Pro and other equipment such as sound interfaces which are more expensive. However, for beginners, the basic podcast equipment will work fine.

Podcast Creation Apps

Mobile apps can be used to create podcast episodes. Many of these apps can also publish the completed episode to your chosen podcast directory. These podcast creation apps vary based on mobile devices.

Backpack Studio App

The Backpack Studio app (formerly Bossjock) for iOS is an all-in-one podcast app. iOS users can record a podcast episode directly from their iOS devices. If you have an Apple iPhone or iPad that uses the lightning connector, you will need a lightning adapter that fits your microphone's adapter type. For instance, most microphones have either a USB or an XLR port, so you will need an adapter for that particular port. Backpack Studio will also allow you to do livestreaming to any station via Icecast or Shoutcast for a fee. With Backpack Studio, you can add in sound effects from cloud storage services such as:

- iCloud
- Dropbox
- Google Drive

You can also record your own sound effects from your iOS device through Backpack Studio or add existing ones from your iOS device. You can also add your show notes directly within the Backpack Studio Notes section to help you stay on topic while recording your episode. Once your sound effects and podcast introduction have been loaded into the soundboard, you can begin recording your episode within the app. Once your episode is finished, you can add your episode title, artist name, and description to help others locate your episode. After entering that information, you can either export your episode to a designated location or save it within the Backpack Studio app. You can also create an audiogram for your podcast within Backpack Studio to share either on YouTube, your classroom, or social media platforms.

Online Audio Recording

Another podcast recording option is online-voice-recorder.com. It is free and can be used within a web browser to make an audio recording. It only requires a microphone and saves the recording as an mp3 or mp4 file. With an easy-to-use interface, you can quickly create an audio recording file that can be imported into another recording application such as Audacity for editing if needed.

Recording Software

Many recording software applications are available to assist you with your podcast. Some are free and open source which works well for limited budgets.

One open source solution is Audacity (Figure 8-4). Audacity is a free cross-platform, open source, digital editing and recording software application available on the Web. It allows users to not only record audio files but also

Chapter 8 | Podcasts

import them. You can also export files into various file formats such as mp3 or mp4. It also allows you to enhance your audio recording's sound quality before exporting it.

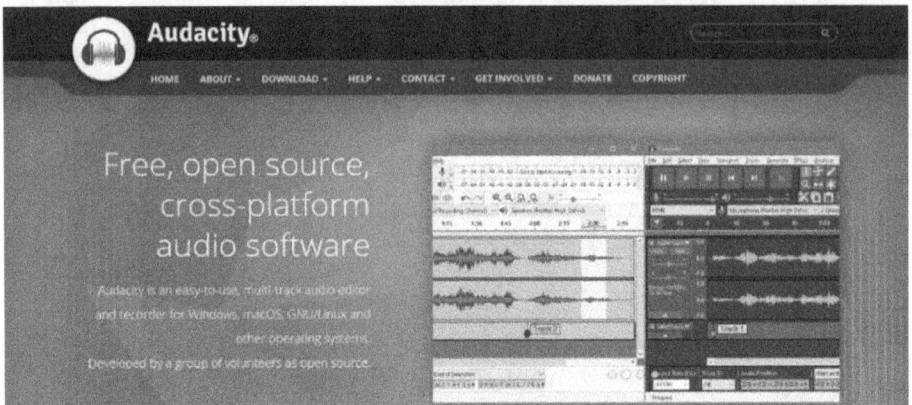

Figure 8-4. Audacity recording software available from www.audacityteam.org/

Another option for Mac and iOS users is GarageBand. It is available for free in the Apple App Store. GarageBand is another all-in-one solution for your podcast needs. With GarageBand, you can record your audio podcast as well as make music for it. GarageBand contains music loops that can be included within your podcast. If you are a musician, you can connect a musical instrument such as a keyboard or guitar to create music to add to your podcast. If your iOS mobile device is newer, it will require an Apple adapter to use equipment with USB ports (Figure 8-5).

Figure 8-5. Adapter for iOS mobile devices that need to use a USB microphone

Podcast Hosting

Podcast directories such as Buzzsprout.com provide free and paid podcast hosting (Figure 8-6). These directories will not only store your podcast files but also generate the RSS feed needed to submit your podcast to other podcast directories. However, free accounts provide limited features. For instance, free plans typically include advertisements that will not be removed until a paid plan is purchased. In addition, many free plans will not allow you to use your uniform resource locator (URL). Your URL provides more branding and marketing opportunities than using a pre-generated URL. Until you are ready to start paying for more advanced podcasting features, it might be a good idea to stick with free podcast hosting. Other podcast hosting that offer free and paid hosting include:

- Anchor.fm
- Podbean.com
- Spreaker.com

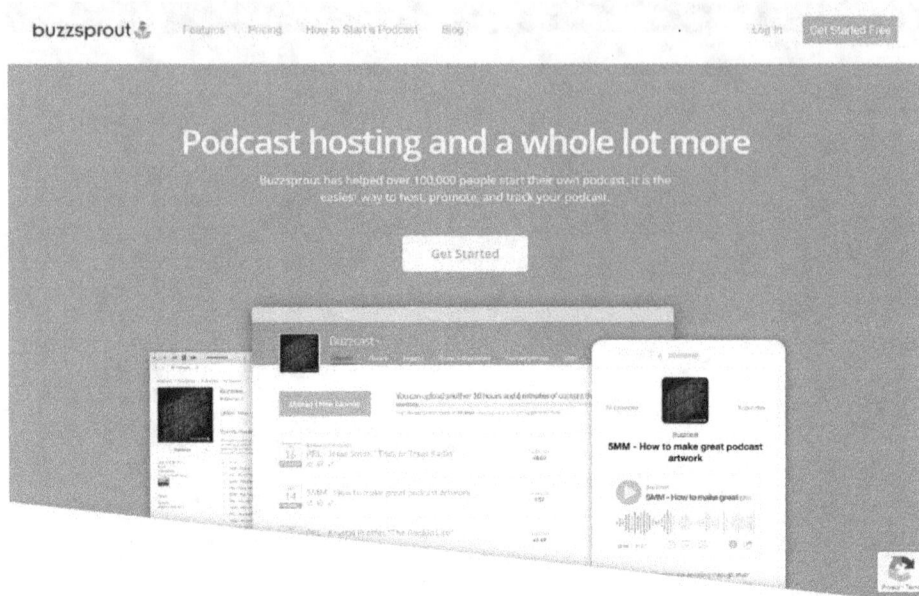

Figure 8-6. Buzzsprout.com provides podcast hosting for podcasters

Once you select your podcast hosting provider, you will need to give your podcast a title, description, artwork, and category. If you are not artistic, Canva can help you create your artwork. Canva provides templates that you can use, or you can create your own design. Some of the other podcast settings you will need to configure include:

- Podcast type
- Website address
- Episode limit
- Keywords
- Artist name
- Contact email address

Once you have recorded and uploaded your podcast episodes, you will need to periodically log in to your podcast hosting to review your podcast stats. These stats will provide valuable insight on your episodes. Some of the insights you will gain about your listeners are:

- Download numbers
- Geographic location

- Devices used to listen
- Apps used to listen

Once you have your podcast's RSS feed, do not forget to submit it to numerous podcast directories to increase your discoverability.

Summary

Podcasts are another tool to help boost your online content while keeping learners engaged. With many podcasts widely available on the Web for free along with being easy to create, they are a perfect fit for any size budget as well as online learning. They also allow learners the flexibility to listen and learn at their convenience and on their preferred mobile and wearable devices. The most important thing to remember is to make incorporating podcasts into your online learning fun and engaging.

CHAPTER 9

Social Media Tools

In the previous chapter, you learned about podcasts and their effectiveness as an online teaching tool. Since they are on demand, learners can easily fit them into their busy schedules and listen at their convenience on their mobile devices. Plenty of podcasts are freely available on any subject. If you cannot find a podcast to meet your learning needs, you can easily and inexpensively create your own with a few simple tools.

Not only are podcasts mobile device friendly but also easily shareable via social media networks. Social media has changed the way people receive and share information as well as connect and build relationships. With social distancing due to Covid-19, social media is being relied on more than ever. Likewise, it has removed geographical boundaries that once prohibited relationship building. Why not take advantage of it within the online learning experience?

The Rise of Social Media

Prior to social media, the primary traditional education communication methods used by educators with learners were mail, phone, and email. These methods could be considered one-way communication because typically the

© Lisa Sims 2021
L. Sims, *Effective Digital Learning*, https://doi.org/10.1007/978-1-4842-6864-3_9

Chapter 9 | Social Media Tools

educators were the ones initiating the contact. Once the contact was initiated, its effectiveness depended on the learner's response.

Although it seems social media exploded on the scene in the mid-2000s, it has been around since 1997. Sixdegrees.com was the first social media site similar to what we have grown accustomed to today. Six degrees of separation has been described as "everyone in the world is connected to someone else through a network of connections that are no more than five links." This concept resembles the social media network LinkedIn which people can connect to others through mutual connections or reach out to make new connections. Although sixdegrees.com had around a million users, it was bought and closed in 2000.

By nature, people are social creatures. One of the selling points for traditional education has been socialization. In an online learning environment, socialization between educators and learners utilizes a variation of the traditional socialization methods via online tools such as web conferencing and social media. According to Pew Internet Research, in 2019, roughly 72% of US adults used at least one social media network.[1] To help learners learn, educators must be willing to meet them where they are rather than where they want them to be. Some examples of popular social media sites today include:

- Facebook
- Instagram
- LinkedIn
- Pinterest
- TikTok
- Twitter
- YouTube

Social media platforms such as Facebook can be used on mobile devices and smartphones which are typically always with you and your learners. When was the last time you left your cell phone home and quickly returned home to retrieve it? Probably more times than you care to admit. By having mobile devices always available, everyone can connect instantly and learn at his or her convenience.

---

[1] www.pewresearch.org/internet/fact-sheet/social-media/

Social Media Feeds

Incorporating social media feeds within online learning can help foster collaboration and keep learners informed of trending news stories. It is a good way to make the connection between the course material and real-world application. For example, incorporating a Twitter feed about a particular industry or subject can supplement the course content (Figure 9-1). Feeds from social media sites such as Facebook and Instagram can also be customized to enhance learners' experiences. Once the feeds are incorporated, they are easy to maintain and update.

Q Search Twitter

COVID-19 · Yesterday

A school reopened. It had to quarantine students within hours.

#DisneyPlus
It's Showtime This August!

Promoted by Disney+

US News · 4 hours ago

Dr. Deborah Birx says COVID-19 is 'extraordinarily widespread' in US

MLB · 3 hours ago

Yoenis Céspedes opts out of the MLB season for COVID-related reasons

Trending with: Cespedes and Mets

COVID-19 · Yesterday

More than 30 crew members of Norwegian cruise ship test positive for COVID-19

Figure 9-1. Twitter feed that can be incorporated into online learning

Facebook Pages

You and other educators probably already have personal social media accounts. However, you probably want to keep these accounts separate to establish boundaries between your professional and personal life. With so many instances of companies firing employees due to the content of their personal Facebook Pages, you might want to take this into consideration. One solution is Facebook Pages. Facebook Pages are separate from your personal account and are typically used by the following:

- Artists
- Public figures
- Businesses
- Brands

They can be used by anyone who wants more ways to engage with customers and target audiences that might not be your Facebook friends. Before creating a Facebook Page, you must have a personal Facebook account or profile. If you decide to create a Facebook Page, you can create a Facebook Page for your course that is frequently updated with interesting videos and links from other websites to supplement the course material and share the page URL with your learners in your course's LMS via announcements or email. By providing real-world, practical examples, learners gain different perspectives on the subject matter. Learners can also connect and engage with you and others by commenting on your posts. They can also share you posts with their Facebook friends, which can increase your exposure and popularity. If learners do not have a Facebook account, they can still access the Facebook Page but will not be able to leave comments. Since it is a public page, anyone on Facebook can see it via the News Feed. You can also encourage learners and others to follow your Facebook Page.

Twitter Chats

Twitter chats, or Tweetchats, are regularly occurring chats hosted on Twitter utilizing the same Twitter account. You can think of them as virtual meetups on Twitter. They happen at the same time on a weekly or monthly basis. The duration can range from 30 minutes to 1 hour. These chats are based on a central theme or topic with its own hashtag. For example, if you wanted to have a Twitter chat about digital learning, you could create a hashtag such as #digitallearningchat that discusses a specific topic of digital learning on the date of the Twitter chat. The key is that every tweet must contain the hashtag to be included in the Twitter chat.

Once you have decided on your subtopic of the main Twitter hashtag, you can begin preparing your questions to engage your learners. Questions typically consist of five to fifteen and begin with "Q1" which stands for question number one. As long as someone knows your Twitter chat hashtag, anyone can join, but he or she must have a Twitter account. Twitter chats are a great way for you and your learners to connect outside of the online learning classroom and engage in meaningful conversations. You can also engage with others to gain a different perspective. It is also a good way to display your expertise while increasing your Twitter followers.

Not sure how to begin? It is a good idea to attend a Twitter chat to get familiar with how it works before planning your Twitter chat. You can find Twitter chats by using the search feature in Twitter and search for #Twitterchats. Once you find a Twitter chat that interests you, participate and take notes of what you liked and did not like so you can structure your Twitter chat for maximum engagement. You can find more information on starting your Twitter chat on the following websites:

- https://sproutsocial.com/insights/twitter-chats/
- https://blog.hubspot.com/blog/tabid/6307/bid/28979/8-steps-to-hosting-a-successful-twitter-chat.aspx

Social Media Groups

Many social media networks such as Facebook and LinkedIn allow users to create groups. These groups can be public or private and be considered similar to an online meetup. As long as a group does not violate the social media platform's term of use policy, a group can be created. A group's permissions and rules are established at creation to determine who can join and what he or she is allowed to do to remain a group member. Similar to Facebook Pages, most social media groups require that you already have a personal profile or account. For example, by creating a Facebook Group, members can participate in the following:

- Create and respond to posts
- View pre-recorded and live videos
- Participate in a Watch Party
- Ask for recommendations
- Take polls
- View photos

Within a Facebook Group, you can also conduct events to gain more exposure. For instance, you could conduct a Facebook Live event on a course topic or have guest speakers that are available only to your group members. You could also add the event to the Facebook Event Calendar for other Facebook users to discover.

LinkedIn is another social media platform that also allows its users to create groups and invite members to join (Figure 9-2). Similar to Facebook Groups, users can perform some of the same functions. These groups are a good way to promote your course material, events, and expertise.

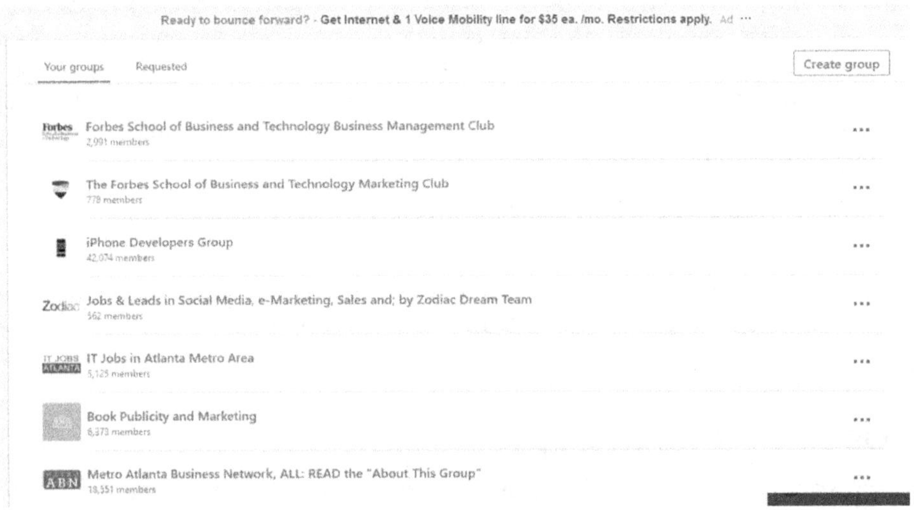

Figure 9-2. Creating LinkedIn Groups is another way to use social media to engage learners

Direct Message (DM)

Many social media networks have built-in messaging communication known as direct messaging, or "DM" for short. Similar to a text message, these direct messages allow users to send messages to people they know or do not know while on social media platforms. This could be another way for learners to connect with educators. For example, Facebook uses Facebook Messenger to allow its users to send other Facebook users messages. However, each user must use Facebook Messenger for it to be effective. Likewise, Twitter, LinkedIn, and Instagram also allow users to send other users messages. What does this mean for you? Learners can reach out to you via direct messages. They can also attach videos, photos, links, and other items to their messages to get help. However, you must be cautious of what you click on to prevent viruses and malware from infecting your devices. Malware can easily be disguised within links, so please be vigilant and attentive as you receive links from students. It is a good practice to have antivirus or malware software installed and frequently updated. Staysafeonline.org provides advice on how to stay safe while on social media.

Facebook Rooms

A new Facebook feature that could be helpful in online learning is Facebook Messenger Rooms. Similar to Zoom, Facebook Messenger Rooms can be used to invite up to 50 Facebook users and non-Facebook users to a video chat without a time limit. Messenger Rooms can be created either in Facebook Messenger or Facebook. Once a Facebook Messenger Room is created, Facebook provides a URL for your Messenger Room which can be shared on other social media networks. With the Covid-19 pandemic, educators and learners have another way to connect while physically apart. However, be aware that the security for Messenger Rooms is not end-to-end encrypted, so be careful what material you share.

Social Media Live Events

Social media networks such as Facebook and Instagram allow users to create live events. Live events allow users to broadcast their video immediately or at a scheduled time for other users to view. For Instagram users, videos and Instagram TV (IGTV) videos can be scheduled for business accounts through Facebook's Creator Studio. Facebook Live Events can be downloaded once completed and uploaded to YouTube for additional exposure. Live events are available to everyone, so you want to be mindful of the information you share.

Summary

With careful planning and research, social media can be incorporated into online learning to increase not only learners' understanding but also engagement. Many tools are available that can help educators meet and greet learners where they are. However, educators must know which social networks will provide the best impact for their learners. Social media has become an essential part of our lives, and we must embrace it. Otherwise, we will miss potential opportunities to connect, share, and collaborate with others no matter where they are located.

CHAPTER 10

Blogs

As you learned in Chapter 9, social media can play a pivotal role in online learning. It provides various channels for educators and learners to connect and engage with the course content. Educators can harness the power of social media to help learners bridge the gap between theory and real-world application.

As technology continues to advance, more tools will become available for educators and learners to use in the online learning environment. These tools will reduce some of the isolation that many online learners experience compared to traditional learning. Blogs are one of those tools currently available but sometimes forgotten.

Blog Basics

Before social media existed, there were blogs. What are blogs? Dictionary. com defines a blog as a "website containing a writer's or group of writers' own experiences, observations, opinions, etc., and often having images and links to other websites." The first blog was created in 1994 by Justin Hall, a Swarthmore College student, on a blogging platform called Links.net.[1] Justin's blog was called Justin's Links from the Underground and provided one of the first guided tours of the Web along with details of his personal life. Previously, blogs such as Justin's were considered the norm in which they were only electronic personal diaries created by one person to share their thoughts and

---

[1] https://online.ndm.edu/news/communication/history-of-blogging/

© Lisa Sims 2021
L. Sims, *Effective Digital Learning*, https://doi.org/10.1007/978-1-4842-6864-3_10

Chapter 10 | Blogs

feelings. Over the years, they have evolved. Today, there are more than 500 million blogs on the Internet.[2]

Today, blogs exist on numerous topics for any audience. These blogs can have one or multiple content creators called bloggers with blog posts consisting of text or multimedia. The blog posts are typically organized in chronological order with the most recent post appearing first. Some of the popular platforms used to create free and paid blogs include:

- WordPress
- Squarespace
- Blogger
- Tumblr
- LiveJournal

Blog directories are available to help locate blogs that might interest you and your learners. They allow for easy searching and are typically organized by categories. One popular blog directory is the Best of the Web Blogs (https://blogs.botw.org) (Figure 10-1).

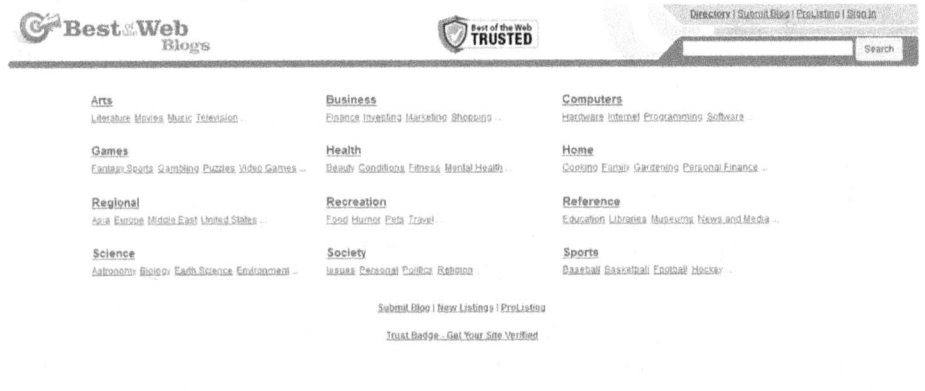

Figure 10-1. A listing of blogs on the Web available from https://blogs.botw.org/

Another resource for locating blogs is www.blogarama.com (Figure 10-2). Blogarama.com provides a listing of over 100,000 blogs on the Web through its easy-to-use search feature. Depending on your topic, you can find a blog to share with your learners and encourage online discussions. You can also find blogs by searching on Google.com.

---

[2]https://hostingtribunal.com/blog/how-many-blogs/#gref

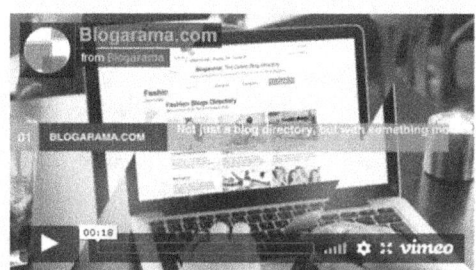

Figure 10-2. Search for blogs on Blogarama.com

Video Blogs (Vlogs)

Most of the blogs you have learned about are the standard textual blogs, but there is another type of blog worth mentioning: video blogs (vlogs). Vlogs, short for video blogs, are blogs that are composed of videos documenting a person's interests or expertise. These videos can be thought of as web episodes. YouTube is the source for most vlogs. All you need to create a vlog is a microphone and a video camera that can consist of one of the following:

- Webcam
- Camcorder
- Digital camera
- Smartphone
- Tablet

Vlogs are quickly becoming the norm. Since these vlogs are visual, they can cater to multiple learning styles of students leading to better engagement.

Advantages of Blogs

Although many people feel that blogs are dead, they are alive and well. Many people still use them to stay updated on information. Compared to websites, people can subscribe to a blog's RSS feed and receive notifications when new content is available. Educators and learners can benefit from blogs.

Updated Frequently

Blogs are frequently updated with content more so than websites. By being periodically updated, Google takes notice and will update its search results with the updated blog posts based on keywords and phrases. As a result, educators can find timely information to supplement course material in their online learning environment.

Encourage Discussion

Engagement in the online learning environment is always an ongoing concern. Utilizing blog posts from outside sources or a blog that you created within your LMS can provide another engagement tool for learners. No two people will have the same perspective on a topic and can benefit from a healthy discussion. Consequently, this can lead to exciting discussions among educators and learners.

Created Easily

If you cannot find a blog that will supplement your course content the way you would like, why not create one? With many free blogging platforms available such as WordPress or Blogger, you can easily create a blog with minimum time and effort. Once created, you can customize your blog's content to enrich your course content. Since it is your blog, you can update it whenever you want.

What kinds of blog posts should you write? Since it is your blog, you have total creative freedom over the blog's subject matter. However, always keep your blog's goal in mind. Your blog posts should align with your course's subject matter as well as your learners' needs. For those course concepts that learners might struggle with, consider writing blog posts that further learners' understanding by answering unanswered questions. Oftentimes, students are afraid to reach out and let you know that they are having difficulty understanding the course material or assignments. Unfortunately, we must anticipate those questions. A blog is a good solution. For instance, you could create a blog post that presents an opposing viewpoint to a particular discussion question or course topic. Within the LMS, you can create a discussion question that requires learners to read the blog post and have them discuss whether they agree or disagree. In either case, a healthy discussion along with different viewpoints can be revealed.

When creating your blog posts, remember that learners have short attention spans. Your posts need to quickly grab and hold their attention. One way to do this is by incorporating quality images within your posts that relate to the blog post topic and grab attention. Chapter 11 will provide some free image resources to help you find engaging and appealing images to include within your blog posts. Next, you want to utilize bullets to make your content easier to read as well as scannable. Long lines of text can intimidate learners, so using bullets along with short paragraphs can help entice and motivate learners to read. Likewise, incorporating videos along with text is another technique to motivate learners to read. You can either create your own videos or use the embed code available from YouTube videos.

Blog Advantages

Since so many blogs already exist on the Web, why should you spend time, effort, and resources creating a new blog? One advantage of having a blog is that you and your learners can easily share posts on social media networks. Sharing your blog posts on social media platforms allows you to establish yourself as an expert, gain followers, and encourage discussions through comments. Compared to other blogs that you do not manage but use their content, you are the owner and control when the blog content is created and released. Lastly, you can customize your blog content to complement your course content. If you decide to use a free blogging platform, remember that the features will be limited. Likewise, you will not be able to customize the blog's URL with your URL without upgrading to a paid version.

Disadvantages of Blogs

Using blogs in online learning benefits learners by helping them further understand the course material. They also encourage collaboration and sharing. However, using blogs in online learning has some disadvantages.

Non-credible Authors

When someone with name recognition creates a blog or blog post, he or she has instant credibility. You feel confident in the post's content and accuracy. Since anyone can create a blog, you must be cautious. If you do not know the blog creator, you are uncertain about his or her expertise. It is a good practice to verify any information before posting it in an online learning environment. Otherwise, it could damage your reputation and hurt your credibility with your learners.

No Control

If you did not create a particular blog, you do not have control over its availability. A blog created by someone else might be discontinued without any advanced notice. It also might experience downtime. When this happens, it will make it unavailable for your learners. Likewise, a blog's URL might be renamed, causing the previous link you shared in your LMS to be invalid.

Summary

Blogs can be a valuable asset in online learning. They are easy to locate and share in any LMS by providing a blog's RSS feed and sharing as an announcement or discussion posts. They can also be included in lectures and assignments. Your course content will determine which blog categories you search to locate blog that complement and supplement your course content. Likewise, they are easy to create and maintain. Learners benefit from blogs because they have another resource to supplement their course material. The blogs also can encourage discussions among educators and learners.

CHAPTER 11

Free Online Resources

In Chapter 10, you learned about blogs and how they can be an invaluable tool to boost engagement and discussion within the online learning environment. With numerous free blogs available on the Web on various topics and constantly growing, you do not need to recreate the wheel unless you want to. If you would like more control, many free blogging software platforms such as Blogger and WordPress are available that can be used to create your own blog.

Every educator needs a good set of tools in his or her toolbox. Unfortunately, due to rising prices and shrinking budgets, some paid tools are too expensive and out of reach. Fortunately, there are many free online resources available that can save you money while promoting learning. You only need to know where to find them.

Tools of Engagement

During Covid-19 virtual learning, engagement is critical. Educators and learners are dealing with a paradigm shift in what learning looks like. Everyone is fatigued in some way and is doing their best to adapt to the best way they know how. With creativity high and budgets low, you as an educator have numerous free options at your disposal but you must know where to look.

© Lisa Sims 2021
L. Sims, *Effective Digital Learning*, https://doi.org/10.1007/978-1-4842-6864-3_11

Chapter 11 | Free Online Resources

Screen Recording

Within the online learning environment, videos compose a majority of the content. Learners tend to be more engaged with videos than written text. Videos also help visual learners understand the content better. To help visual learners as you learned about learning styles in Chapter 4, you can experiment with free screen recording tools. Although there are many screen recording tools available, let's take a look at a few popular ones.

Screencastify

Screencastify is a recording tool available as an extension only within the Google Chrome browser (Figure 11-1). It can be installed within your browser from the Chrome Web Store. It is compatible with most devices including Chromebooks that use the Google Chrome browser except for mobile devices.

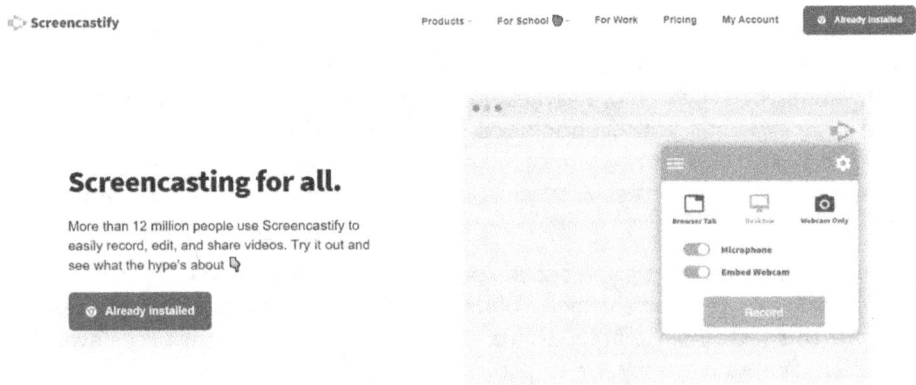

Figure 11-1. Screencastify is available at www.screencastify.com

You can use it to record one of the following:
- Desktop
- Browser Tab
- Webcam only

Whichever recording type you choose, you can provide software demonstrations, presentations, and more to increase learners' understanding. Likewise, you could use the webcam only option to record a lecture, provide assignment feedback, or offer motivational words. The options are limited.

Effective Digital Learning

Regardless of the recording type you select, the free version has a 5-minute limit per recording. You can always upgrade to the paid version, but the free version should be sufficient for you and your learners' needs.

Screencast-O-Matic

Another free screen recording application to consider is Screencast-O-Matic (Figure 11-2). It allows you to create recordings on a Mac or Windows computer, Chromebook, and iOS and Android devices. Compared to Screencastify, free account recordings have a 15-minute limit. Once you are done recording, it allows you to use its editor to edit it and share your video. Unlike Screencastify, it is a stand-alone application and can be installed from www.screencast-o-matic.com.

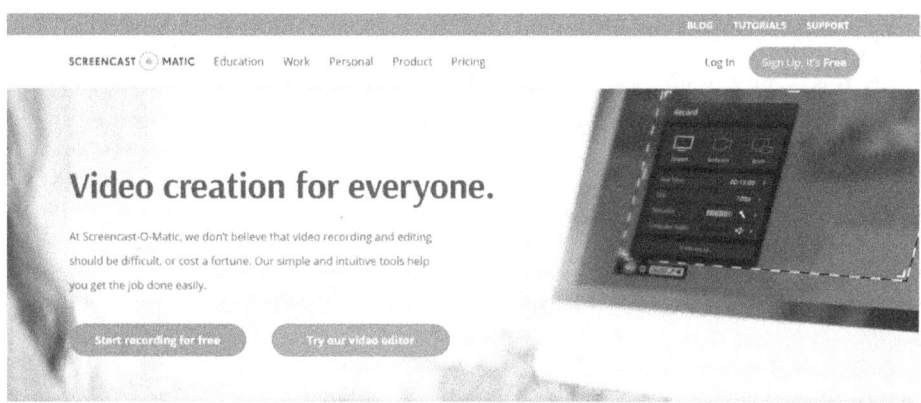

Figure 11-2. Screencast-O-Matic allows you to create recordings for free

Images

Who has not needed to find an image to enhance their content but did not want to pay for it? No one. Selecting the right images can mean the difference between keeping learners' attentions and losing them. With all the image repositories available on the Web, one should not be forgotten: Google Images.

Google Images

One repository that you might have unintentionally overlooked is Google Images (Figure 11-3).

Figure 11-3. Google Images is an image repository for all types of images

Keeping with the same simple design as Google.com, Google Images is also easy to use. Google Images (https://images.google.com) allows you to apply advanced search criteria to find images with usage rights that allow you to freely use, share, or modify for commercial or noncommercial use. To apply this, you would select Settings ➤ Advanced Search (Figure 11-4).

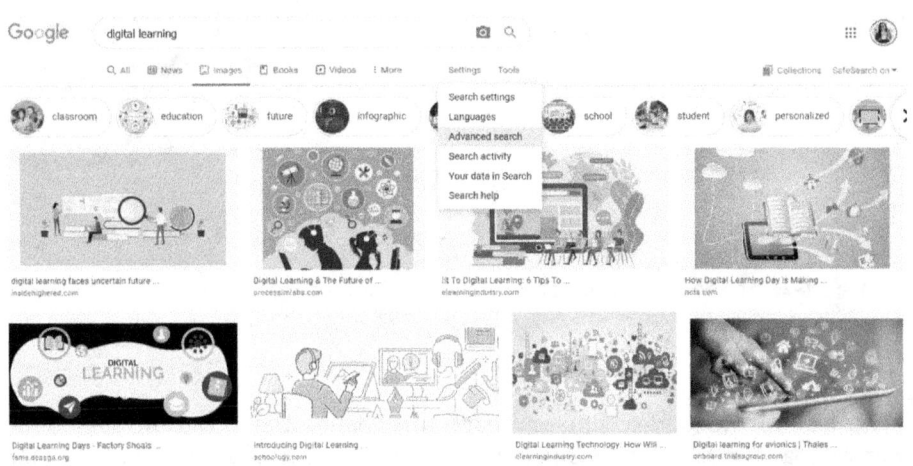

Figure 11-4. Using settings to apply advanced search features in Google

Think of the time and money you could save by first searching Google Images.

Unsplash

Another resource for free images is Unsplash.com (Figure 11-5). It is free to join and the images are free to use. Also, the website is easy to use and provides many categories to choose from. If you are using Google Slides for your presentations, you can use the Google Slides add-on and the Unsplash iPad app to locate images.

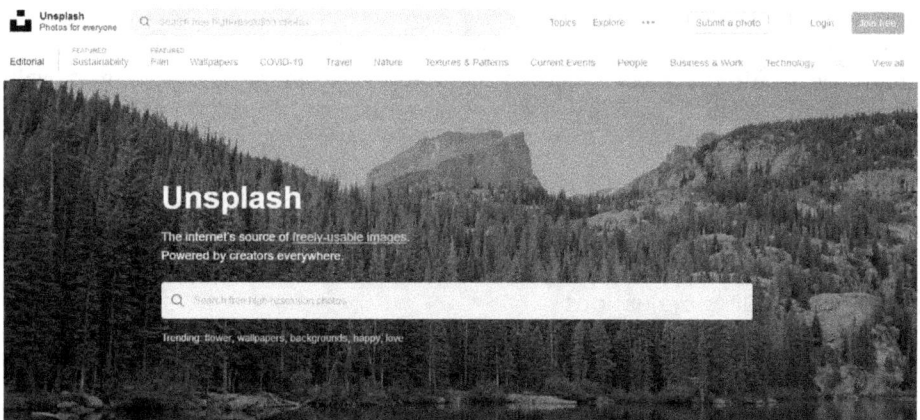

Figure 11-5. Unsplash (https://unsplash.com) is another free image repository

Pexels

If you need more images to support your virtual learning content, you should visit Pexels.com. All images on Pexels.com are free to use and do not require attribution. It also provides videos. Not only can you incorporate these images within your course content materials such as announcements and discussions but also on your social media platforms and blog posts. The possibilities are endless and are only limited by your creativity and imagination.

Online Forms

Being able to use online forms in your virtual learning environment can save you time and allow you to receive responses faster. Many options are available to help you, but there is a free resource that you should not overlook: Google Forms.

Google Forms

Google Forms allow you to create online forms for personal or business use. To get started using Google Forms, you need a Google Account which is free to create for individuals. If you work for an organization, you should verify whether Google Workspace is available. If not, your organization would need to sign up for Google Workspace for enhanced security and team collaboration.

Within Google Forms, many templates are available to help you get started. If you do not find a template that meets your needs, you can create your own. The Google Forms interface is easy to use and implement within your virtual classrooms. All you need to do is include a URL in your course materials. Some of the types of forms you can create include:

- Surveys
- Quizzes
- Event registration
- Course evaluations
- Event feedback

You are not limited in what forms you can create. Whatever you can visualize, you can design within Google Forms. Forms can be a good way to gain feedback from your learners to help you make adjustments in your learning.

Cloud Storage

As you are creating your content for your courses, you want to make sure you have access to your materials from any device. You never know when the unexpected will occur, so having a backup in place is a good idea. Cloud storage is the solution. With cloud storage, your information is stored "in the cloud (on a computer on the Web)," making it accessible from any Internet-connected device.

Google Drive

One cloud storage solution used by many is Google Drive (Figure 11-6). It is easy to use on any type of device. It also has a mobile app that is available on both iOS and Android mobile devices. To use Google Drive, you need a Google Account which is free. At the time of this writing, Google Drive provides 15GB of free storage that is shared between Google Drive, Gmail, and Google Photos. If you need more space, you can always upgrade to a paid plan. Your organization might have a plan that offers unlimited storage so it is a good idea to find out. You can also share files and folders with others within Google Drive which can save time and paper and promote collaboration.

Effective Digital Learning | 99

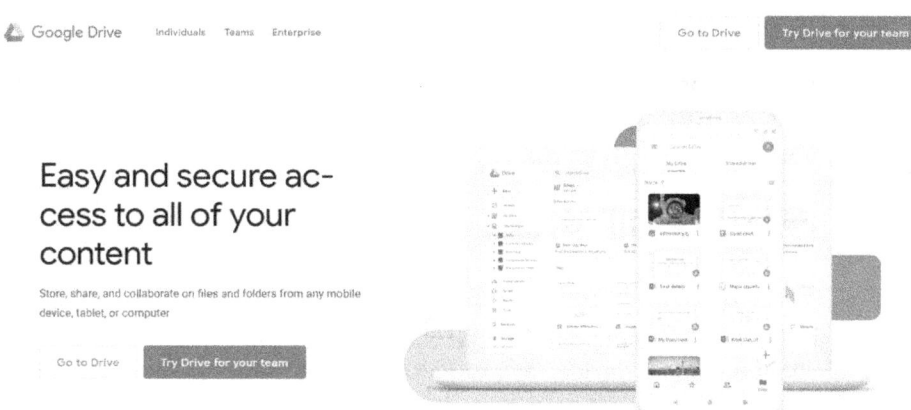

Figure 11-6. Google Drive (www.google.com/drive) offers cloud storage for your needs

Dropbox

Another contender for free cloud storage is Dropbox (Figure 11-7). Dropbox offers a free basic plan with 2GB of cloud storage space for your files. Compared to Google Drive, this is small, but it is an option. To get more storage, you would have to upgrade to a paid plan.

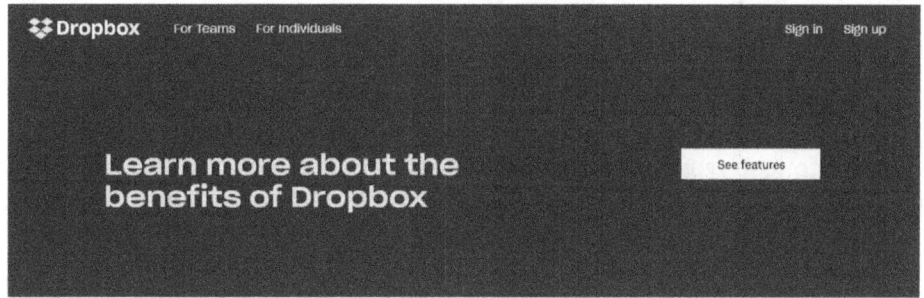

Find the right Dropbox plan for you

Figure 11-7. Dropbox (www.dropbox.com) is another cloud storage solution for your online needs

OneDrive

If you have a Microsoft account, you can use OneDrive. OneDrive works on the following devices:

- Windows PCs and laptops with Windows 10
- Windows Surface tablet
- Xbox One Console

It includes 5GB of free file storage. One feature of OneDrive is that it automatically backs up your files to the cloud. It also syncs them so that they are accessible from any device. You can also share files from OneDrive. Most organizations use Office 365 so you already have access to OneDrive. You would need to inquire about your storage capacity.

Utilities

Outside of the tools that have already been mentioned, some important utilities can help you create engaging virtual learning content. They can also help you present a more professional image.

Grammarly

How many times have you received some type of written communication that was not only difficult to read but also understand? Probably more times than you care to remember. Imagine how your online learners feel when they receive poorly written communication. Poorly written communication causes learners to lose trust and confidence in educators as well as their expertise. Thoughts and ideas that are not properly written cannot be easily communicated.

Grammarly is a web-based application that can help you improve the effectiveness and professionalism of your writing. It offers a free and paid version. To use it, you can either copy your written text and paste it into the Grammarly website or upload a file to Grammarly to review. A Grammarly add-on can also be installed and run within Microsoft Word as well as your browser. Once Grammarly has your text, it will review it for not only grammatical errors but also other areas to produce clear and concise writing. It also can review your emails, social media posts, and more. By using Grammarly, you can make sure that your course content is free from errors and presents you in the best possible way. It also helps your learners build trust and confidence in you and your expertise. Grammarly can be found at www.grammarly.com.

Snipping Tool

Although it is not an online resource, it is a free and valuable resource for educators. For PC users with Windows 7 and later, a preinstalled app is available called the Snipping Tool. The Snipping Tool provides the ability to perform screen captures. It can be opened by typing Snipping Tool in the Search box of the Windows taskbar. Once opened, you can snip or capture information in one of the following forms:

- Free-form snip
- Rectangular snip
- Window snip
- Full-screen snip

After your snip is completed, you can save it to your PC to include in your course materials such as lectures, documents, announcements, discussions, assignments, and more.

Summary

As you have seen, free does not always mean bad or inferior. With so many free resources available on the Web for virtual learning, it would be difficult to list them all in this book. Hopefully, you have seen that many of these free resources are comparable to their paid counterparts. Now that you know about some of these resources, you can start creating an exciting online learning experience that your learners will never forget. You also will not forget it because you will have saved money in the process.

CHAPTER 12

Testing Online Learning

Chapter 11 discussed various free online resources to not only maximize your teaching experience but also boost student engagement. Some educators might view free online resources as inferior compared to paid options, but that is not always the case. With rising prices along with shrinking budgets and paychecks, some fee-based learning resources are too expensive. As a result, you must either research creative workaround solutions or find free alternatives.

Once you have found your resources, familiarized yourself with them, and incorporated them into your course materials within your LMS, you might feel that you are finished. Unfortunately, you are not. You have another crucial step: testing. Despite your best efforts, unexpected things happen. As Murphy's Law warns us, *"Anything that can go wrong will go wrong."* Proper testing decreases the likelihood of Murphy's Law.

Why Testing Is Important

In an ideal world, technology would automatically work as intended. Unfortunately, this is not the case particularly in online learning. As schools transitioned from traditional in-person learning to online learning during the Covid-19 pandemic, many technology issues arose. Due to increased system

© Lisa Sims 2021
L. Sims, *Effective Digital Learning*, https://doi.org/10.1007/978-1-4842-6864-3_12

demand, students and educators were unable to access their LMSs. Many students lacked Internet service or computers to complete their course work. You probably have personal war stories to share about your experience. Although a pandemic is an extraordinary circumstance, prior testing still needs to be performed to anticipate and prepare for these circumstances.

Types of Testing

Testing online learning management systems is critical. Nothing is worse than learners encountering preventable errors at the onset or during a course. These preventable errors can create a bad first impression for learners that can affect their attitude not only toward online learning but also about you and the course. It is a good practice to have more than one person to perform various testing functions on various computers and mobile devices. However, if you do not have others available to assist with testing, you can still perform effective testing. Before we begin discussing testing, you need to be aware of the two types of testing you will perform in your virtual learning environment: usability and performance.

Usability Testing

Usability testing evaluates how you, students, and any potential users use and interact with the LMS or virtual learning environment. Your testing will answer questions such as

- Can users log in to the system?
- Can users access the LMS through computers and mobile devices?
- Can users easily navigate the LMS?
- Can users easily find what they need?
- Are users able to submit information successfully and accurately?
- Are certain user roles prohibited from performing certain tasks?
- What file formats are learners able to upload?
- Can screen readers read the course content?
- Is alternate text available for images?
- Is closed captioning available within videos?

To perform usability testing in a virtual learning environment, you or the LMS administrator will need to create a user with a student role within the LMS. This will allow you to see the LMS from the student's perspective along with performance testing. Many learning management systems have a student view option that will make this easy. Once you are in student view, you will be able to navigate the LMS to perform testing that answers the questions listed previously.

At the end of your course or term, do not forget to survey your learners about their learning experience. These surveys can provide valuable feedback as well as identify improvement areas. Many LMSs provide the ability to offer surveys. If not, you can easily create free surveys and include the link in an announcement or email that can be sent to learners using the following tools:

- SurveyMonkey – www.surveymonkey.com
- Google Forms – www.google.com/forms/about/

Usability testing is an ongoing process. It must be periodically done to ensure that learners are receiving a positive learning experience. Additional resources that can provide information on LMS testing include:

- QA Source – https://blog.qasource.com/test-a-learning-management-system
- eLearning Industry – https://elearningindustry.com/ways-measure-learning-management-system-lms-reliability-check-fulfills-business-goals

Performance Testing

Performance testing involves testing a system's infrastructure to verify that it can handle a certain number of concurrent users without crashing. This infrastructure consists of servers, networks, Internet connection, and more. For instance, prior performance testing of schools' infrastructures and bandwidths before shifting learning solely online could have detected and corrected many of the issues and frustration encountered by students and parents ahead of time.

Along with performance testing, schools' or organizations' invisible infrastructures that store the LMS should periodically be tested for scalability. Scalability refers to a system's ability to grow or scale beyond its current size or state as needs change without encountering problems. One misconception of online learning is that it only involves having a computer and Internet service. For educators and students, this is true. However, the technology involved behind the scenes to create a seamless online learning experience requires much more technology.

Performance testing also identifies potential issues before they become real issues. It is always a good practice for schools and organizations to proactively test rather than reactively test. Your success as an educator and your student's success depend on it. Nothing is more discouraging for teachers and students than to encounter technical problems at the beginning of online learning. If these problems are not quickly corrected, they can potentially snowball into even bigger problems. As a result, both educators and students can become frustrated and unmotivated. Likewise, ongoing problems can also affect not only your reputation as an educator but also your school's or organization's reputation. Whether it was your fault or not, students typically blame the educators first and the school or organization second.

Security Testing

Security concerns have become commonplace, especially in the online classroom. We all have heard or experienced security breaches that have occurred in the online classroom. For instance, educators must apply the strictest of security settings for their Zoom sessions to prevent Zoombombing. Zoombombing occurs on the Zoom web conferencing application once an unauthorized user gains access to a Zoom session and does or says something offensive. The main objective is to disrupt the session. Think of how this could affect impressionable young learners. The effects could be devastating. Oftentimes, the threats originate from outside of the online classroom while others are from within. In any case, both of these unwarranted threats must be anticipated and swiftly handled. Within the LMS, it is a good practice to grant roles the least level of security to prevent any potential security concerns. Oftentimes, this is handled by your LMS administrator.

Content Testing

Since most educators are not LMS administrators, they can only control those things that are within their role's permissions. Content is one of those areas. Educators provide most, if not all, of the content in the LMS for the online learning experience. As a result, you want to make sure that you have verified the accuracy of your information. Other tasks to perform to test your content include:

- Spell-check all your content
- Verify all hyperlinks work
- Verify all images display correctly
- Provide downloadable material as PDFs
- Format references according to the American Psychological Association (APA) format

Summary

Testing in the online learning environment should not be considered as an afterthought. It is just as vital as all the other online learning components. Testing is not a one-time task. It must be periodically done to save not only time but also headaches for administrators, educators, and students. Inadequate testing can have devastating effects on the overall online learning experience.

CHAPTER 13

Marketing Online Learning

In the previous chapter, you explored the importance of testing your online learning components. Although testing is typically handled by a learning management system administrator, as an educator, you also must test your learning content for not only accuracy but comprehension. Not testing your content could expose potential errors that might negatively affect not only your reputation as an educator but also your school's reputation. It is critical that you verify various aspects of your students' experiences so that it is as error-free as possible. Likewise, you want to verify that all students can access and view your content as you intended.

Once you have tested your online learning materials, it is time to spread the word about your courses. Whether you work for a school with its own Marketing Department or you are working independently, you need to market your expertise and your courses.

Getting the Word Out

What good is it to have expertise and course offerings if no one knows that either exist? If you are hoping people discover you by happenstance, you are mistaken. You have to be proactive and help people find out about your

Chapter 13 | Marketing Online Learning

expertise and course offerings. Today, there are many resources and tools available that can assist you with this. Most of these resources are free and only require an investment of your time. Let's take a look at some.

Word of Mouth Marketing

Although it has been around for a long time, it is still one of the best marketing strategies available. When people have a positive experience, they love to share it with others. With social media, word of mouth marketing has gotten faster and reaches farther than it previously did. Word of mouth marketing is a verbal or written endorsement of a product or service from a trusted source to a potential customer. Its value is priceless and costs you nothing. Nielsen.com reported that 92% of people trust recommendations from friends and family over any other type of advertising.[1] What are you waiting for? Start telling your friends and family about your expertise and course offerings. You can even encourage them to take a course that you teach. Whatever you need to do to create your own brand ambassadors, do it. For instance, use Canva to create some images that contain information about your expertise and courses that you can provide to your brand ambassadors to share on their social media platforms. The more followers they have provides more opportunities for exposure for you. You could also create a video using one of the free resources mentioned in this book and post it on YouTube as well as your social media networks. Likewise, you can share the YouTube link with your brand ambassadors to share with their followers. It will take some time for you to see results but it will pay huge dividends. Consistency is key.

Social Media

Social media has propelled the reach of word of mouth marketing. With social media mobile apps such as Facebook, Twitter, Instagram, LinkedIn, and others at the fingertips of consumers, it is easier to share information with others than ever before. If you do not have a social media presence, you need to immediately begin to create one. Think about which social media platforms your target audience uses and make sure you are using those as well. A few resources to help you identify social media demographics include:

- HubSpot – https://blog.hubspot.com/marketing/state-of-social-media-demographics
- Marketing Charts – www.marketingcharts.com/digital/social-media-108184

---

[1] www.nielsen.com/us/en/insights/report/2012/global-trust-in-advertising-and-brand-messages-2/

- Social Media Examiner – www.socialmediaexaminer.com
- Kronos.com – https://khoros.com/resources/social-media-demographics-guide
- Pew Research Center – www.pewresearch.org

As you are creating your social media profile names, make sure that they possess the following four characteristics:

- Easy to remember
- Easy to spell
- All the same across all platforms
- Provide some insight into what you do

By incorporating these four characteristics, you save potential learners time in locating you and your online learning offerings when they perform searches either on Google or social media platforms. Your social media profiles also need to include keywords that potential learners would search for to find courses such as yours. A good free resource to help with this is the Google Keyword Planner. It is apart of Google Ads. Google Keyword Planner allows you to search for words and phrases that people use to search on Google. It displays the search volume for those words and phrases and also provides suggestions. By using Google Keyword Planner as your guide, you will have a road map as to what keywords you should target to get results.

Facebook Page

In addition to your personal social media accounts, a Facebook Page is quickly becoming a necessity. A Facebook Page is used by individuals and businesses to promote their products and services rather than using a personal Facebook account (Figure 13-1).

Chapter 13 | Marketing Online Learning

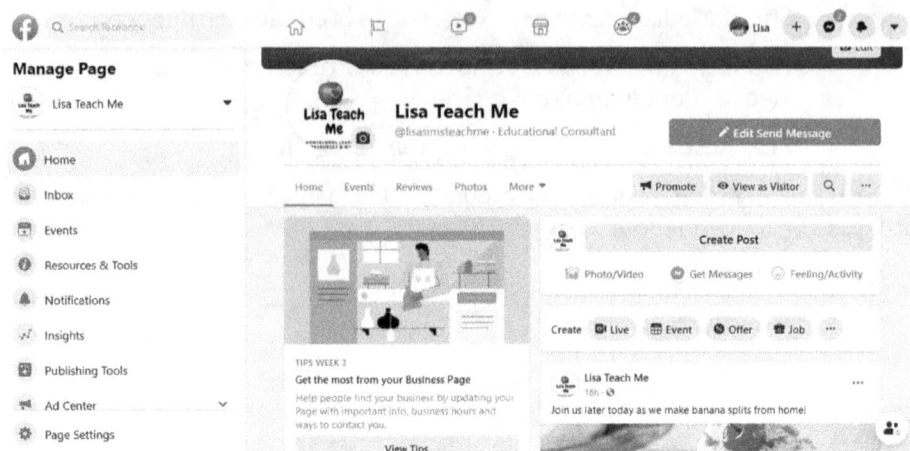

Figure 13-1. Using a Facebook Page to help promote your online learning

A Facebook Page offers the same features as a personal account along with detailed analytics of your page's performance. When analyzed and applied, this information can improve your marketing efforts. With your Facebook Page, you can also post images, website URLs, videos, and more. You can also conduct Facebook Live sessions where you teach on a particular topic on a designated day and time. Your Facebook Live will be available in the public news feed for everyone to see. It is a good practice to create an event so that it is added to the Facebook Event Calendar for everyone to see. Once the Facebook Live event is over, the recording is saved to your Facebook Page. You can also download your Facebook Live video and post it on other sites such as YouTube and social media platforms. Other social media platforms such as LinkedIn, Periscope, Instagram, and TikTok will also allow you to perform a live broadcast.

YouTube

What better place to market yourself and your online courses than YouTube? According to hootsuite.com, YouTube is the second most preferred platform for watching video on TV screens among 18- to 34-year-olds.[2] Pew Research also identified YouTube as the most popular platform in America.[3] To showcase your expertise, why not create a YouTube channel and upload short tutorial videos teaching your course material? Viewers receive a glimpse into your teaching style while learning more about you and what you have to offer. As you are creating your videos, make sure that you include keywords in your

---

[2] https://blog.hootsuite.com/youtube-stats-marketers/#user
[3] www.pewresearch.org/fact-tank/2019/12/04/10-facts-about-americans-and-youtube/

video title and description to make it easier for learners to find either when searching on YouTube or Google. You also want to make sure that you include your social media handles within your YouTube videos to gain followers. It is all about making it easy for learners to find and follow you.

Another great thing about YouTube is that you can embed your YouTube video into your website/blog or easily share your video's URL across multiple social media platforms. This is another way that you can use one marketing asset for multiple marketing purposes for maximum impact.

Conferences

Due to Covid-19, most in-person conferences have shifted to virtual events such as webinars. Regardless of their format, they still provide excellent opportunities to not only learn but also network with others. A strong network can help you reach audiences that previously were not possible. Not sure where to find conferences?

When attending online events, do not forget to network. Although networking looks different in virtual events compared to in-person events, it is still important. As the old adage goes, "It's not what you know but who you know." You must be creative in your approach. For instance, most virtual event platforms offer attendees a chat feature. You can utilize the chat feature to introduce yourself and provide a link to your website or LinkedIn profile to connect with others. For virtual conferences that allow you to create a profile, do not miss this opportunity to not only include an informative biography that includes your areas of expertise but also links to your social media accounts and online courses website. Never miss a chance to promote yourself, your website, and your online courses. You might not get a second chance. Some resources to look for virtual conferences include:

- www.Edweb.net
- www.linkedin.com
- www.facebook.com
- www.eventbrite.com
- www.meetup.com
- www.google.com

Guest Appearances

To spread the word about your expertise and online course offerings, look for ways to be a guest on various media platforms. For example, you could contact some BlogTalkRadio hosts or podcasters with shows aligned with your online course offerings to be a guest. By doing this, you are not only providing the host with content but also expanding your marketing reach to their listeners. Likewise, you will gain free publicity because the host will promote you on his or her show's page and social media networks. This promotion can include your image, biography, website link, social media links, and more. You will also be able to promote the guest appearance on your social media networks and website before and after the show.

Being a guest on a webinar is another way to promote your expertise and online courses. Since Covid-19 imposed social distancing, everyone is conducting webinars and looking for guests. Why not you? Why not find some companies hosting webinars on your subject matter and ask to be a guest? All they can say is no. Once you become a webinar guest or panelist and the webinar is over, you have a recording to add to your media kit to help you market your yourself and your online courses. Do not forget that you can create your own webinars using tools such as Zoom, record yourself teaching a topic, and save the recording to share on any of your social media platforms.

Website/Blog

If you have a website or blog, it is the perfect place to market yourself and your expertise. If you do not have a website or blog, Chapter 10 can help you get started. In any case, it is important that you have one or both. Since you own these, you can update them with new content at your convenience. For instance, you can create a media area page on your website or blog that links to all your previous guest appearances. When you are looking for guest appearances, you can use this page as your portfolio to showcase your talent to potential podcast and webinar hosts. You can also share this link on your social media networks. As mentioned in Chapter 10, you can also create blog posts based on your expertise that can be easily shared on social media networks.

Using social media is good but it is a good idea to have your own website or blog. Although social media is here to stay, some of the networks have experienced unexpected downtime. For many, social media networks are their only promotion and selling source. By having your own website, you have complete control and ownership of it that can be used to promote yourself and your expertise 24 hours a day, 7 days a week. Don't forget to utilize the Google Keyword Planner to research keywords that will help the right visitors find you.

Another website promotion technique that you can use is an email sign-up form. You can provide free information applicable to your expertise in the form of a newsletter. Visitors can provide their email address in exchange for the newsletter. Mailchimp (www.mailchimp.com) is a free resource that can help you with this. It is easy to include on your website. Likewise, it will provide you with a link that can be shared on your social media networks. By having an email sign-up form on your website or shareable link, you are building a list of potential customers for your online courses that you can market to on a consistent basis.

Once you have a website or blog running, you must make sure that you are frequently reviewing its analytics. Analytics provide insightful information on your website's or blog's performance. Some of the information consists of the following:

- Number of visitors
- Geographic location of visitors
- Duration of visitor's visit
- Pages visitors visited
- Devices used to find your website

This information is available from your website or blog hosting provider. Another good analytics tool to include in your website or blog is Google Analytics. Google Analytics is a free tool that provides valuable insight about your website or blog to help improve its performance and marketing reach. It can be accessed through your web browser or via the Google Analytics app for iOS and Android devices. You can sign up for Google Analytics with your Google Account by visiting https://analytics.google.com. After your account has been created, click Admin located at the bottom of the page to begin setting up your website or blog. Once on the Admin tab, click the Create Account button for new website or blog (Figure 13-2).

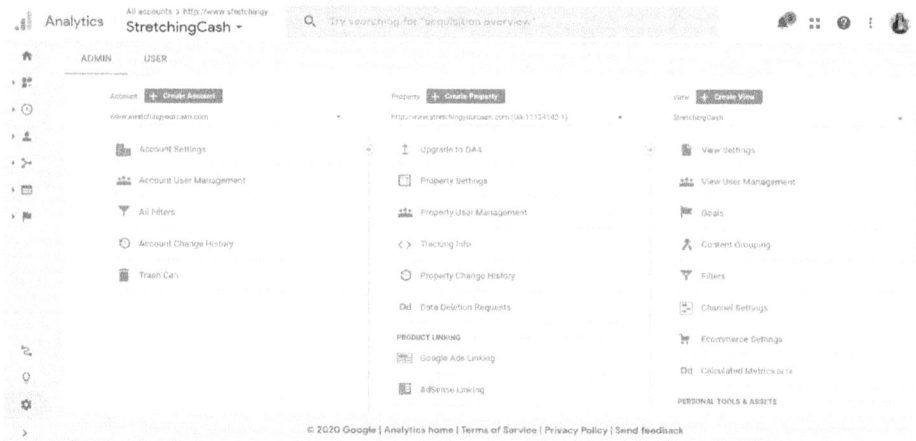

Figure 13-2. Setting up Google Analytics for your website or blog

Chapter 13 | Marketing Online Learning

You will set up an Account name and a Property name for your website along with your business information. Once you have completed the information, you will click the Create button. You must accept the Google Analytics Terms of Service Agreement along with the Additional Terms Applicable to Data Share With Google before continuing. After agreeing to the terms, you will be presented with a screen that allows you to select whether you want to track an app or website. You will select website (Figure 13-3).

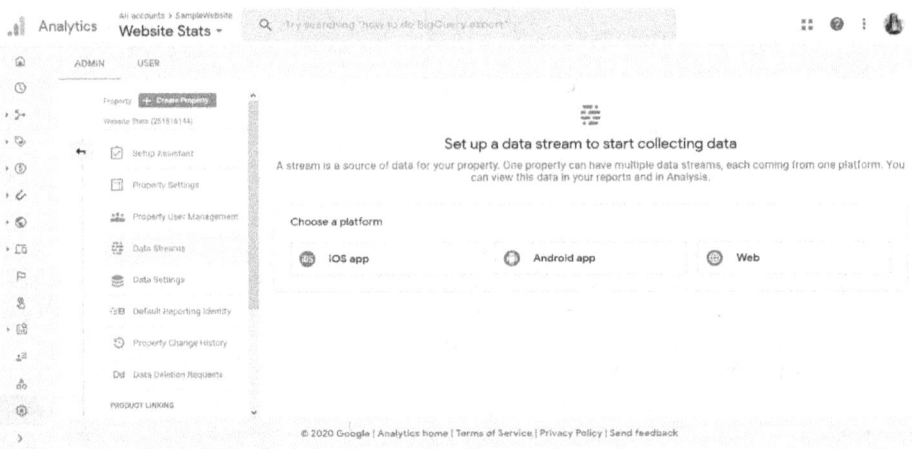

Figure 13-3. Selecting your data stream in Google Analytics

After selecting the website option, you can provide your website address. Once you provide your website, you will receive your code that needs to be copied into the <head> section of every HTML web page you want to measure (Figure 13-4).

Effective Digital Learning | 117

Figure 13-4. Global Site Tag code to insert into web pages for tracking

If this seems confusing, do not worry. Within Google Analytics, tutorials and other help resources are available to get you started. Once set up, you can review your website's Google Analytics using either your web browser or the Google Analytics mobile app. Likewise, you can make changes to your website to improve its marketing reach. Lastly, you can always make changes within Google Analytics to what website information is measured.

Podcasts

As mentioned in Chapter 8, podcasts are not only a good online learning tool but also a good marketing tool. Not only can you promote your expertise but you can also market yourself. For instance, within your podcast's introduction, you can provide your subscribers with information about any upcoming online courses, guest appearances, and other events. You can also remind subscribers about the same information in your podcast's closing. Since you are the creator, you control each episode's content as well as its publishing schedule. Always post your podcast episodes on your social media networks and embed your podcast player on your website. Not sure how to do this? Your podcast host will provide you with this information. As with your website, do not forget to frequently review your stats.

Summary

To be effective at marketing yourself and your online courses, you must clearly identify your target audience. Once you have your target audience, you can create your marketing strategy or marketing plan to effectively reach them. As you are working your marketing plan, remember that marketing must be done often and consistently to be effective and see results. Furthermore, you must measure your marketing efforts and make any necessary adjustments to improve your marketing reach. Always remember that there is no silver bullet to marketing. You must continue to fire your bullets in the right places to hit your target.

CHAPTER 14

Before You Go

In Chapter 13, you explored the various ways to not only market your courses but also market yourself. It is up to you to let the world know who you are, along with your expertise. Contrary to what people think, nothing happens by chance. Newton's Third Law of Motion says it this way: *For every action, there is an equal and opposite reaction.* You provide the action through various methods. Unfortunately, those that discover you might never take a course. However, they can still help spread the word about you.

There is no better time than the present to start prioritizing your marketing efforts. You are your biggest marketer. It can make the difference between being discovered or not. With social media, it has become easier to spark people's interests and spread the word about yourself. Next, your students are also one of your most prominent marketers. They have experienced your courses and your expertise and can tell others. Depending on their ages, you might need to empower their parents with tools to provide reviews or testimonials about you and your courses. Do not be afraid to solicit their help.

Final Thoughts

Being an online educator is not easy. It also is not for the faint at heart. There will be many long hours of prepping, teaching, tutoring, and grading. However, it can be rewarding. If you are transitioning to online learning from traditional learning due to Covid-19, you will need some time to develop your online teaching style and rhythm. It will not happen overnight. Go easy on yourself and give yourself a break. As you become more comfortable in the virtual

© Lisa Sims 2021
L. Sims, *Effective Digital Learning*, https://doi.org/10.1007/978-1-4842-6864-3_14

environment, it will get easier. Nothing is as accurate as the saying *"Everyone was a novice before becoming an expert."* The same applies to online teaching. Online learning is a marathon and not a sprint. However, there are some things that you can do to help yourself improve along the way.

Professional Development

As an educator, you never stop learning. With technology advancing at a rapid rate, there is always something new to learn. You must be willing to embrace it and incorporate it within your courses. In this information age that we currently live in, information is readily available at our fingertips via our mobile devices or voice commands with Siri or Alexa. We can easily experience information overload. However, it is a good idea to invest in yourself and gain new skills and resources to keep you marketable. Many free resources available on the Web include:

- Edutopia.com
- Edweb.net
- Edu.google.com
- Edx.org
- Microsoft.com/en-us/education/remote-learning
- Udemy.com

Attending webinars and online conferences is another way to increase your professional development. During this Covid-19 pandemic, many conferences have shifted online and are being offered for free or at a reduced cost. Why not take advantage of these? If you register for a webinar or conference and cannot attend at the designated time, recordings are typically made available to attendees after the event.

Technology

Technology continues to evolve every day. What is hot today will be obsolete in a year or less. While you are investing in your professional development, it is also imperative that you invest in hardware and software. Mobile apps and cloud-based applications have quickly become the norm. As an educator, you must know how to use them to increase not only your efficiency but also productivity. Likewise, it would help if you strived to stay current on online learning technology tools and trends. These tools can help you improve in the online learning environment. Some useful podcast resources available include:

- Faculty Seminars in Online Teaching
- Level Up Your Course

- Online Learning Podcast
- The eLearning Coach
- The Good Practice
- The Online Course Coach

Social Media

In the past, you had to purchase tickets for events with some of the famous thought leaders to gain information and insight. Social media revolutionized this. Today, you have access to these same experts and thought leaders and can learn from them as they share their knowledge. The best part is that it is *free*! Not sure whom to follow? Here are some eLearning thought leaders to get you started:

- Julie Dirksen, author of *Design for How People Learn*
- Jane Bozarth, author of *eLearning Solutions on a Shoestring*
- David Anderson, Community Manager at Articulate
- Christopher Pappas, eLearning expert extraordinaire and founder of eLearningIndustry.com
- Clark Quinn, learning consultant, co-author of The Serious eLearning Manifesto

Books

Most of our great leaders are readers. The same should apply to educators. New books are published daily that can help you enhance your skills as an online educator. Many libraries offer free ebook platforms to read books on mobile devices. Likewise, you can create a free account at pdfdrive.com and add ebooks to your account to read. Amazon Kindle also offers free Kindle ebooks that can be read on a Kindle or the Kindle app. The books are out there. You must know where to look.

Summary

As you have read through the chapters of this book, I hope that you gained more insight as you read along than when you first started. There is so much more to online learning that all of it would not fit within one single book. However, this book is a good introduction that can help you get started. You already have a willingness to learn. Otherwise, you would not have purchased this book. Likewise, you already have what it takes to be a good teacher. Your objective is to transform those characteristics into the online learning

Chapter 14 | Before You Go

environment. During these challenging times, it will not be easy, but it is possible. I believe in you, but the most critical question is: Do you believe in yourself?

Feel free to follow and message me on social media to let me know how you enjoyed the book and how it helped you.

As I close, I want to inspire you with this eLearning quote by Christopher Palm:

> eLearning shouldn't be a casual joy ride on a Sunday afternoon with the cruise control engaged. The sole purpose of eLearning is to teach.

Now get online and teach!

Index

A
Apple Keynote application, 51–53

B
Blogs
    advantages, 89
    Blogarama.com, 88, 89
    bloggers, 88
    directories, 88
    disadvantages
        control over, 92
        non-credible authors, 91
    engagement tool, 90
    Justin's Links, 87
    technology, 87
    updated frequently, 90
    video blogs (vlogs), 89

C, D
Content is king
    basics, 27
    benefits, 27
    elements, 28
    goals, 30, 32
    learning types, 29
    price/learning materials, 30
    website content accessible, 29

E
Equipment, Online learning, 9
    accessories, 14
    antivirus software, 12
    cloud-based storage options, 13
    graphic design software, 13, 14
    hardware, 10
    headset with microphone, 14–16
    Internet connection, 14
    Microsoft Office 365, 11
    PDFs reader, 13
    printer, 11
    scanner, 11
    software, 11
    technology, 9
    webcam, 16, 17

F
Free online resources, 93
    cloud storage, 98
        Dropbox, 99
        Google Drive, 98
    engagement, 93
    Google Forms, 98
    grammatical errors, 100
    image repositories
        Google Images, 95, 96
        Pixels, 97
        unsplash iPad app, 97
    OneDrive, 100
    online forms, 97
    screen recording tools, 94
        Screencastify, 94, 95
        Screencast-O-Matic, 95
    snipping tool, 101
    utilities, 100

Index

G, H, I, J, K
Google Slides, 50, 51

L
Learning management system (LMS), 3, 33
- assets, 34
- benefit, 41
- categories, 35
- free option, 39, 40
- institutions, 34
- limitation, 41
- Moodle open source, 37–39
- open source platforms, 36
- proprietary/commercial platforms, 36
- requirements, 34, 35

LibreOffice Impress, 53

M, N
Marketing department, 109
- characteristics, 111
- demographics, 110
- Facebook Page, 112
- guest appearances, 113
- in-person conferences, 113
- podcast player, 117
- social media, 110
- virtual conferences, 113
- website/blog
  - account button, 115
  - data stream, 116
  - global site tag code, 117
  - insightful information, 115
  - social media networks, 114
  - website/shareable link, 115
- word of mouth marketing, 110
- YouTube, 112

O
Online learning
- asynchronous, 5
- benefits, 5
- considerations
  - digital divide, 6
  - needs learners, 7
  - quality, 6
- flexibility, 5
- Google search results, 4
- mobile device technology, 6
- money saver, 5
- public education
  - definition, 1
  - eLearning/virtual learning, 2
  - evolution, 2
  - history, 1
- time saver, 5
- virtual classroom, 5

P, Q
Performance testing, 105, 106

Planning process
- benefits, 19
- Facebook Pages, 24
- mindset, 20
- online teaching skills and knowledge, 21
- organization system, 20
- purpose, 19
- self-care tips, 25
- time management, 22, 23
- work/teach, 24

Podcasts
- advantages, 70, 71
- audacity recording software, 74
- audio recording application, 73
- backpack studio app, 73
- component, 67
- creation equipment, 72
- free and paid hosting, 75–77
- Google Play Store, 69
- iOS devices, 68
- iPodder, 67
- mobile apps, 72
- planning, 71
- quality microphone, 72
- recording software applications, 73–75
- RSS feed program, 69
- uniform resource locator (URL), 75–77
- video, 71

PowerPoint presentations, 45, 47–50

Presentation tool, 43
- animations, 46
- Apple Keynote application, 51–53
- Google Slides, 50
- KISS principle, 45

Index

LibreOffice Impress, 53
materials, 43, 44
music connects and
    energizes, 47
PowerPoint presentations, 47–49
Prezi, 49, 50
quality images, 46
reducing clutter, 45
slide decks, 44
strategies, 45
transitions, 46
websites, 47

Prezi presentation tool, 49, 50
Professional development, 120

R

Really simple syndication (RSS), 69

S

Security testing, 106
Social media tools
    communication methods, 79, 80
    direct messaging (DM), 84
    Facebook Page, 82
    LinkedIn Groups creation, 84
    live events, 85
    messenger rooms, 85
    mobile device, 79
    traditional socialization methods, 80
    Twitter chats/Tweetchats, 82, 83
    Twitter feed, 81

T, U

Testing learning resources, 103
    content, 106
    management systems, 104
    online learning, 103
    performance testing, 105
    security concerns, 106
    usability testing, 104, 105

V

Video blogs (vlogs), 89

W, X, Y, Z

Webinars, 55
    advantages, 56
    AnyMeeting, 64
    delivery strategies, 57
        breakout rooms, 59
        gamification, 60
        polls, 58
        questions/answers, 59
        style/tone, 57
        videos, 59
        whiteboard feature, 58
    Google Meet, 65, 66
    lectures, workshops, and seminars, 56
    livestreaming, 60, 61
    Microsoft Teams, 63, 64
    requirements, 57
    video conferencing software, 56
    zoom, 61–63

GPSR Compliance

The European Union's (EU) General Product Safety Regulation (GPSR) is a set of rules that requires consumer products to be safe and our obligations to ensure this.

If you have any concerns about our products, you can contact us on

ProductSafety@springernature.com

In case Publisher is established outside the EU, the EU authorized representative is:

Springer Nature Customer Service Center GmbH
Europaplatz 3
69115 Heidelberg, Germany

www.ingramcontent.com/pod-product-compliance
Lightning Source LLC
LaVergne TN
LVHW010343260326
834688LV00036B/856